ADVANCE PRAISE FOR

THE E-BUSINESS BOOK: A STEP-BY-STEP GUIDE TO E-COMMERCE AND BEYOND

by Dayle M. Smith

"Dayle Smith's e-business book is **an essential, hands-on primer** for any Internet executive."

STEVE WESTLY
Former Senior Vice President
eBay

"A **practical guide for those entering the Internet world for the first time or for those who didn't get it right the first time around.** Just reading a few chapters of this book could **make a difference between a start-up making it or not making it** in this slowing economy."

HEATHER L. MCFARLANE
Consultant
Korn/Ferry International

"**Easy to follow, well organized, and grounded in realism**—this is quite a book."

BILL BLASE
President–External Affairs
Pacific Bell

"Dayle Smith brings business planning to the e-commerce era. It's about time! **This practical guide could have saved millions for start-up e-businesses.**"

WILLIAM J. MOODY
Former Vice President of Global Services
AT&T

"Questions in the front, answers right away—this is my kind of book! I spend 15 to 20 percent of my reading time on e-commerce: **This is a guide that works. More than just information, this book is about application, plus resources.** Dayle will save you the cost of the book if you use the wealth of new e-commerce resource sites she provides in *The E-Business Book.*"

J. WILLIAM NEWTON
President/CEO
Norcal Mutual Insurance Co.

"*The E-Business Book* offers **keen, up-to-date insights** and **practical guidance for entrepreneurs** and seasoned business operators alike. The book provides fascinating examples of Internet initiatives, sorts fact from fiction, and is **likely to save any business decision-maker days of research time.**"

W. ANDERSON BARNES
CEO
Barnes & Company

"In the past year, it has become clear that implementing an e-commerce solution is not as easy as building a Web site. The book **guides you through the process of building an e-business and the key metrics in evaluating your Web site.** This is a **must-read** for every beginning entrepreneur or for anyone who needs a refresher course on getting back to the basics."

JUDITH BITTERLI
Chairman and CEO
Powered, Inc.

The E-Business Book

The E-Business Book

A STEP-BY-STEP GUIDE TO E-COMMERCE AND BEYOND

Dayle M. Smith

Viva Books Private Limited
New Delhi • Mumbai • Chennai • Kolkata

First Indian Edition 2003

Viva Books Private Limited

- 4262/3 Ansari Road, New Delhi 110002.
  e-mail : viva@mantraonline.com
- 215-216 New Apollo Estate, Mogra Lane, Andheri (E), Mumbai 400069
  e-mail : vivabooks@mantraonline.com
- 7 Aziz Mulk Seventh Street, Thousand Lights, Chennai 600006
  e-mail : vivachennai@mantraonline.com
- 6-A Rifle Range Road, Kolkata 700019
  e-mail : vivakolkata@mantraonline.com

Visit us at **www.vivagroupindia.com**

Published by Arrangement with
Bloomberg Press
100 Business Park Drive
P.O. Box 888
Princeton, NJ 08542 0888
USA

ISBN 81-7649-337-6

Published by Vinod Vasishtha for Viva Books Private Limited, 4262/3 Ansari Road, New Delhi - 110 002 and printed at Raj Press, New Delhi - 110 012.

To my daughters, Lauren Elizabeth and Madeleine Alexis, for whom e-business is already the rule rather than the exception

Foreword

IF WE HAD ANY DOUBTS, THE FIRST YEAR OF THE NEW century made it clear that this is a time of consolidation and rethinking for e-business in all its aspects. The nova stars of most dot-com companies spawned in the late 1990s have now blinked out of existence or faded to the point of invisibility. The e-business survivors in this great shake-out deserve our admiration and study.

The E-Business Book: A Step-by-Step Guide to E-Commerce and Beyond undertakes that study in a lively, informed, and insightful way. Dayle Smith's steps to e-business success are precisely what most dot-com companies need in the first place—cogent business planning that combines the best of Old Economy thinking with the imaginative vision of the New Economy. Above all, the author is realistic about both the challenges and potentials of e-business ventures. She recognizes (along with most investors at this point) that low barriers to business entry inevitably portend ferocious competition and high failure rates among e-business startups. She also has a sane perspective on the projected profitability of even the most prominent e-business contenders.

This is not to say the author has lost her own enthusiasm for the basic proposition of e-business and Internet commerce. Far from it. She simply refuses to perpetuate hope in the form of hype. Instead, her book guides the reader skillfully and accurately behind the mask of conflicting opinions, statistics, and claims that has become the tortured face of e-business at present. The realities the book exposes make up a fascinating story that is both cautionary and attractive. The easiest way to lose your shirt in e-business, Smith rightly asserts, is to ignore principles of basic business planning and operations. Hundreds of thousands of singed e-business investors certainly will grant her point.

But *The E-Business Book* is valuable for reasons beyond its wise analysis of the perils and pitfalls of e-business. The author creates here a road map for companies and individuals who want to start and run e-businesses the right way—or repair the mistakes of their previous efforts. A major portion of Smith's pages are devoted to a topic often ignored in e-business publications: how to grow and maintain your e-business after its exciting debut on the Internet. Her road map depicts the entire e-business journey to success.

Dayle Smith is confident, as I am, that the factors of speed, price, quality, availability, and service possible through e-business will see it through these stormy times and ensure its eventual dominance in consumer and business-to-business commerce. The current sagging stock prices of many e-business giants may, in a year or two, be viewed retrospectively as the buying opportunity of the decade. New technologies, including revolutionary ways to manage and measure knowledge itself, will add to the market dynamism and durability of e-businesses.

In sum, the ultimate message that emerges from Smith's superb book is "keep the faith—but with your eyes wide open." The future for e-business is bright, and all the brighter for the light Smith shines on the route to e-business success.

THOMAS J. HOUSEL, PH.D.
Academic Program Director
Information and Operations Management Department
Marshall School of Business, University of Southern California

ACKNOWLEDGMENTS

MANY INDIVIDUALS AND ORGANIZATIONS WERE INFLUENTIAL in shaping the topics, information, and insights of this book. To all, I offer heartfelt thanks: Sheryl Barker, Undergraduate Director, School of Business, University of San Francisco; Art Bell, Ph.D.; Dan Blakley, Ph.D.; Karl Boedecker, Ph.D.; Mark Cannice, Ph.D.; Alicia Esterkamp, M.B.A. Candidate; Carol Graham, Ph.D.; Nick Imparato, Ph.D.; Vincent Leger, MBA; Bill Murray, Ph.D.; Eugene Muscat, Senior Associate Dean, School of Business, University of San Francisco; Denis Neilson, Associate Dean of the School of Business, University of San Francisco; Gary Williams, Ph.D., Dean of the School of Business, University of San Francisco; and a host of e-business executives and managers at more than fifty companies, including Charles Schwab & Co., Citicorp, Agilent Technologies, Pacific Bell, Johnson & Johnson, eBay.com, Amazon.com, Fogdog.com, Webvan.com, eToys.com, and many others. Special thanks go to my talented editors at Bloomberg Press, Kathleen Peterson and Tracy Tait, and to the entire staff.

Introduction

IT'S ALL TOO EASY TO LOSE MONEY AND TIME ATTEMPTing to build or enhance an e-business site on the Internet. *The E-Business Book: A Step-by-Step Guide to E-Commerce and Beyond* tells the story of both the promises and the problems of getting your e-business up and running. Finding your way in a relatively straight line from the old economy of bricks-and-mortar business to the new shores of e-business takes courage, work, and not a little luck.

The E-Business Book unfolds as twelve linked steps for e-business success. Let's take a bird's-eye view of that path before beginning our journey together.

Step 1: Learn what it means to join the e-business revolution.

The sea change toward e-business has been called the most significant business development since the

Industrial Revolution more than two centuries ago. In setting your sails for these largely uncharted waters, you will naturally want to know how others, past and present, have fared in their e-business efforts. This step gives you the opportunity to see your e-business concept in the context of our times. You will be able to benchmark your efforts against those who are moving more quickly or more slowly—and you will learn as well from those who have abandoned ship entirely.

Step 2: Find your unique place in the e-business crowd.

Equipped with an understanding of the e-business revolution, you are better able to locate your own place amid the many hundreds of new e-business Web sites arriving on the Internet each day. What makes your e-business stand out? Why will customers click on your Web site in preference to others? Once they try your site for the first time, what will entice them to stay? These are questions that lie at the heart of your e-business success. A clear vision of your specialness—your competitive advantage—gives you a foundation upon which to build your e-business empire, large or small.

Step 3: Shape your e-business idea.

Whether your e-business idea is simple or quite complex, you will need to personally undertake the work involved in finishing the phrases "and then..." as well as "what if...." This step shows you how to play out mental scenarios in the roles of the e-business owner and customer. In later steps, you will soon be engaged in programming (or out-sourcing your programming) based on your detailed plans for your Web site and e-business. That vision of a new business comes primarily from you, the company founder. Others may end up blowing your horn, but you're writing the score.

Step 4: Investigate your e-business competition.

Are you a "me-too" business or an absolute original? Certainly there's nothing wrong with following a profitable path blazed by someone else, within legal limits. Many successful "me-too" e-businesses have purposely positioned themselves as second-wave enterprises, allowing first-wave businesses to create a marketplace and run headlong into barriers to market entry. There's also much to be said for absolutely original e-business ideas, especially those that can't be quickly cloned by others.

In either case, you will want to know as much as possible about your competition. This step shows techniques to get you past the PR surface of a competitor's business to what makes it tick. By understanding your competitors' successes and failures, you move toward your own set of winning strategies.

Step 5: Formalize and conceptually test your business idea.

Your e-business runs just fine in your head. Now set it to paper to see if the gears still mesh smoothly. In this essential phase of formalization, testing, revision, and confirmation, Step 5 presents the fundamentals of writing an e-business plan. You will need this document not only for approaching investors, if needed, but also to orient possible partners or employees to the details of your concept. Many e-business developers find that the writing of the business plan is an excellent way to discover previously hidden flaws and pitfalls in the e-business concept and process. As stated so aptly by T. S. Eliot, "Between the conception and the reality falls the shadow." Setting down all significant aspects of how the business works helps to expose unexamined assumptions and inadvertent oversights.

Testing the completed business plan does not require full-scale deployment of the e-business Web site. General Motors, by analogy, did not build a huge automobile manufacturing plant in order to determine whether its cars would sell. This step shows relatively inexpensive ways to "circuit-test" a business plan without exposing its proprietary ideas or unduly delaying its progress toward the marketplace.

Step 6: Protect your e-business concept.

It's yours, and it works! But will your e-business concept remain yours, especially after it demonstrates its success to the world? This step explains the importance of knowledge management, including knowledge protection, to your e-business enterprise. Unlike a traditional factory, your e-business hums along by virtue of its ideas, not its physical machinery. Those ideas can be stolen by a would-be competitor much more easily than can massive extrusion devices and complicated assembly lines. Patent and copyright law for the Internet and e-business is rapidly being written (and tested) so that your intellectual property doesn't end up in someone else's backyard.

Step 7: Build a fast, functional Web site.

The technology of Web site construction has progressed sufficiently in recent months so that any person of reasonable intelligence, given a few hours with appropriate manuals and software, can get a Web site up and running. This step will show you how to do so but also will give reasons why you may decide to outsource this work. Dollars are seldom so well spent as your investment in a Web site that can grow as your business grows, adjust rapidly to unexpected market changes, and serve your customers quickly and reliably. This step shows several options for using professional services in developing your Web site.

Step 8: Market your e-business.

Your e-business star twinkles for the first time in the business firmament. But what about those bazillion other stars filling the sky? This step shows proven ways to market your products, your services, and your Web site itself.

Step 9: Find a trading community to support your e-business.

Building e-business alliances and finding membership in healthy e-business communities that are already drawing substantial customer traffic are both sound business practices. This step explores business-to-consumer malls as well as business-to-business trade communities.

Step 10: Build your e-business team.

This step shows sophisticated but easy-to-practice ways to avoid pitfalls in building your team along with new techniques to hire the right people and meld them into a winning team.

Step 11: Manage your e-business team.

This continuation of the human side of e-business focuses on how to motivate your crew to do their best work, encourage their integrity, and manage knowledge and change in your enterprise. If this sounds a bit like a mini-M.B.A. program, you're right—but always applied to the new needs of e-business.

Step 12: Evaluate and enhance your business model and Web site design.

Based on regular inspections of your Web site and observations about changes on the Internet, you will probably find it necessary to make changes in your business model and Web site. This final step suggests that you steer away from the "repair" mentality and adopt instead an "enhancement" perspective. A repair, after all, keeps bad things from recurring. An enhancement goes beyond a repair in helping good things to happen. Various avenues for Web site and business model enhancement are offered in this step, each with explanations and examples showing how you can apply these forward-thinking measures to your e-business. Suggestions are also included for tracking customer satisfaction with your Web site and responding effectively to customer feedback.

Finally, three appendices provide guidance to additional resources. **Appendix A** contains *Entrepreneur Magazine*'s May 2000 annotated list of the best Web sites for your business. **Appendix B** lists e-mail addresses for foreign embassies in the United States as well as U.S. embassies abroad. These contacts can help you spark global business for your Web site and also help you comply with trade and customs regulations for countries with whom you do e-business. Last, **Appendix C** presents emerging guidelines from the Web Accessibility Initiative, which seeks to make the use of the Internet more user-friendly for people with disabilities. Complying with these guidelines may make your e-business less vulnerable to lawsuits questioning your compliance with the Americans with Disabilities Act.

Thank heavens for Netiquette, with its insistence on plain talk. Authors writing about e-business can now relax and simply tell it straight to their readers. In fact, by using my e-mail (smithdm@usfca.edu), you can tell it straight right back to me while or after you read this book. I welcome your comments and questions.

1

STEP 1

Learn What It Means to Join the E-Business Revolution

W HEN IT COMES TO RECENT DEVelopments in e-business, Shakespeare's phrase fits well: "This is the winter of our discontent." Billions of dollars in IPO funding and start-up capital have gone down the rabbit hole, perhaps never to return for most dot-com companies and investors. Prominent dot-com bankruptcies punctuate the financial news each week. Back when this book went to press, hundreds of e-business retailers, including the biggest names, were holding their corporate breath in hopes of a profitable holiday period. The great majority of such firms spawned in the late 1990s didn't make it to holiday season 2000. Even Pets.com had thrown in the towel, leaving its TV sock puppet as one of its few saleable assets.

Emotionally, the timing may be difficult for a new book on how to start, run, and profit from an e-business. Many of us have been bruised in one way or another by the collapse of dot-coms. *But, intellectually, the time could not be better to rethink and retool.* As the following chapters seek to demonstrate, the essential nexus of price, speed of delivery, availability of product, shopping convenience, and 24/7 customer service continues to make e-business a potent contender for retail dollars in the years ahead. "The idea still makes sense," most e-entrepreneurs and investors assert. "We just have to focus on execution." That focus on execution and strategy can be found in virtually each page of *The E-Business Book.*

Surely the Web is the future for commerce in all forms. In its February 28, 2000, issue *Business Week* quotes Andrew Bartels, a small-business analyst at Giga Information Group in Cambridge, Massachusetts: "A small business has to be on the Internet, the way it has to be in the Yellow Pages.

It's that simple." The Web, concludes the article, "is becoming the first stop for comparison shopping and research. If your product or service isn't listed, you're missing out."

But your reasons for establishing a Web presence for your business must not be built on the shifting sands of other people's opinions. To the best of my ability, this book will give the facts about how money is made and wasted on the Internet, who is making a killing and who is being killed, and how you can take rational steps to e-business success rather than make a madcap leap into the abyss.

Examining Our Internet Assumptions

YOU PROBABLY KNOW MUCH ABOUT THE INTERNET AND USE IT regularly for business and pleasure. You have no doubt developed beliefs and attitudes, pro and con, about the e-businesses you visit on the Net. On the basis of those beliefs and attitudes, you are now contemplating (or already undertaking) a significant investment of time, personal energy, and money devoted to an e-business venture. Your efforts, in fact, may involve a substantial risk of your own money or someone else's.

Before you pick out the wallpaper for this rising structure, your e-empire, let's take a moment to examine its foundations. The goal here is to locate solid ground on which to build a successful e-business. To inspect the footings of your Internet assumptions, please jot down quick "True" or "False" answers to each question on the following Internet Quiz:

1 **T or F:** A majority of American households are now connected to the Internet.

2 **T or F:** Most small businesses in America have an Internet site of some kind.

3 **T or F:** In 2000, Americans spent about 25¢ of their retail shopping dollar through Internet channels.

4 **T or F:** Most major retailers now have e-business sites where you can buy their products directly.

5 **T or F:** In 2000, American companies spent about 20¢ of their advertising dollar for ads on the Internet.

6 **T or F:** The majority of households using the Internet made at least one e-business purchase in 2000.

7 **T or F:** Search engines (such as Yahoo!, Lycos, and Goto) are the primary way by which people find the Internet sites they seek.

8 **T or F:** Telephone-related companies (Pacific Bell, GTE, Bellsouth, AT&T, and others) have the greatest market share as Internet Service Providers (ISPs).

9 **T or F:** Of all Internet users throughout the world, most specify a language other than English as their primary language.

10 **T or F:** Lycos, Excite, AOL, Goto, InfoSeek, and Netscape are the major players in the search engine arena.

AND NOW THE RESULTS, PLEASE

READY TO GRADE YOUR QUIZ? I'LL MAKE YOUR TASK EASY: THE answers to all ten questions are "False." Here are the details you will want to consider in understanding why your assumptions may have gone south while the facts about e-business went in another direction entirely.

- **Question 1:** Are most households reached by the Web? Not at all. At present, 38 percent of American households are linked to the Web. That number is growing, but not as quickly as other media such as television caught on with the American public. Household access to the Internet went from 0 percent in 1990 to 38 percent in 2000. In the same number of years in the period 1950 to 1960, household television access went from 9 percent to 87 percent.
- **Question 2:** How do small businesses feel about having their own Internet sites? In a late-1999 survey conducted by International Communication Research, two-thirds of small businesses said they saw no benefit to creating Web pages. In 2000, there were some 7.7 million small businesses in the United States. Only 2.7 million had Web sites. Fewer still (1.6 million) were using Web sites for commercial as opposed to informational or advertising purposes.
- **Question 3:** Did Americans spend much of their retail dollar on the Web? Not by a long shot. In 1999, according to economist Robert Samuelson, spending on retail e-busi-

ness was "puny...it amounted to less than 0.5 percent of U.S. consumer spending."

- **Question 4:** Have traditional retailers embraced the Web? Although it is true that the majority of "name" retailers have Web sites, these sites are by and large "info sites" with corporate addresses, contact numbers, and so forth. Relatively few major retailers provide an actual commercial site where a customer can buy product without visiting a store.
- **Question 5:** Has a lion's share of advertising shifted to the Web? Not even a mouse's share, according to a Universal McCann estimate reported in *Newsweek*, January 24, 2000: "In 1999, Internet ads amounted to $1.8 billion out of total U.S. advertising of $215 billion." Put another way, the Web accounts for less than 0.5 percent of U.S. advertising expenditures.
- **Question 6:** Did households linked to the Internet make purchases there? *Forbes* recently reported that less than one out of ten homes linked to the Internet have made a purchase there.
- **Question 7:** Are search engines the primary way to bring a potential customer to your site? According to May 2000 statistics compiled by SuperStats.com, only about 8 percent of Web users found their way to sites using search engines. Instead, 40 percent used other Web sites as their main finding method.
- **Question 8:** Are telephone-related companies the big gorillas in the Internet Service Provider arena? In spite of their omnipresent and aggressive advertising, the market share of all telephone-related companies *combined* is only about 8 percent of the total ISP market—and pales in comparison to AOL's 16 percent market share.
- **Question 9:** Are non-English speakers a substantial audience among the world's 90 million Internet users? Not according to their chosen-language setting on their computers' operating systems. More than 83 percent of Internet users select English as their primary language for Internet communication, with Chinese a far-distant second at 1.6 percent.
- **Question 10:** Are Lycos, Excite, AOL, Goto, InfoSeek, and Netscape the major search-engine players in terms of market share? Hardly. Yahoo! holds more than 25 percent of the market, compared to low-single-digit shares for the rest, with the exception of AOL, which holds a 13 percent market share.

MAKING SENSE OF YOUR RESULTS

THERE'S NO MAGNA CUM LAUDE SCORE ON THIS QUIZ. ITS payoff lies in the revelation that not all that glitters is gold, whether in the California of 1849 or the Internet of the new century. These answers should also help you conclude that the Internet is still in its infancy as an e-business force within the American and world economies.

The most defensible broad generalization about e-business on the Internet right at this moment is hardly rosy: Most companies now attempting to do business on the Internet are not seeing a profit for their investment, although many hope to see better results in the future. One noted economist recently called e-business on the Internet "a capitalist charity. Almost everything on it is being given away or sold at a loss."

If you were under a different impression, it's certainly not your fault. There's an "information war" raging now between data gatherers and vendors with a vested interest in presenting the Web in the most glowing, growing terms possible and the research of more detached Internet observers, many of them academics, who are struggling mightily to get a fix on "hard numbers." The truth, as usual, probably lies somewhere in between.

Do not be surprised in reading this book, therefore, when seemingly contradictory or conflicting data is put forward by various sources claiming to have a finger on the pulse of the Internet. Here's a snapshot of the Web, based on April/May 2000 reporting from such sources.

1 How often do people bother to click through on banner ads? In the mid-1990s, 2.5 people out of every 100 clicked on a banner ad. That number had dropped precipitously to 0.36 during March 2000, according to Nielsen NetRatings.

2 Has such poor banner response affected advertising revenues? According to the Internet Advertising Bureau, Internet advertising revenues more than doubled in 1999 compared to 1998, reaching $4.62 billion. Most of this advertising, says AdRelevance, can be attributed to business-to-business online advertising.

3 By May 2000, about 2.8 million small businesses were

transacting on the Internet, up from 1.8 million in 1998. Access Markets International Partners finds that U.S. small business spending on online transactions and purchases grew by more than 1,000 percent, rising from $2 billion in 1998 to $25 billion in 1999.

4 Almost two in three Americans over the age of twelve have access to the Internet, and half of those go online every day, according to ACNielsen.

5 Forrester Research Group predicts that global e-commerce will be worth $6.9 trillion by 2004 and that 89 percent of all online transactions will be made by only twelve countries. Among that number, for example, more than 15 million Italians were expected to be online by 2001, according to Between ICT Brokers. Continental Research estimates that British Internet users numbered about 14 million in 2000, a significant emerging market with no language barriers to U.S. sites.

6 Sources disagree on how much Web traffic (as reflected in average time online per user, number of Web users in toto, expenditures online per Web user, number of "hits" per site, total revenue for small businesses online, and so forth) can be laid at the door (or the back door) of the tens of thousands of pornography sites now on the Web. No matter what one's personal feelings about such sites, it is undeniable that they represent a major economic engine driving the popularity of the Internet. Some sources recommend that one subtract 30 percent from any statistical data about business on the Web if you want to discount the pornography element.

SO THE NUMBERS PRESENT A MIXED BAG. HUGE INTERNET revenues seem just around the corner, but many small businesses earning little or nothing on the Web hope they can survive to see that corner. Total advertising expenditures are up while advertising techniques such as banner ads are an increasing failure. Does this information throw a wet blanket on e-business efforts on the Internet? No—it just points up a few of the facts that you must confront before you get pushed along in line to board the trains for the great gold rush of the 2000s.

The key to e-business success lies in learning to step

around the pitfalls that have swallowed up so much capital and human effort in recent years. Toward that end, this book is designed along a path of twelve steps. If you're ready, let's begin along that path at a cautious walking pace instead of the mad dash so common today among Internet wanna-be's—and often so economically disastrous.

A Crowded Playing Field

FOR ONCE, OSCAR WILDE WAS WRONG. HE OPINED THAT "nothing succeeds like excess." In the case of dot-com companies, their excessive numbers and more excessive rhetoric have caused a distinct backlash among consumers. If your spouse quits his or her job to join a dot-com, you now hold your breath. If your son or daughter leaves college to work for a dot-com, you bite your tongue. Especially after the dramatic downward revaluation of many Internet stocks that began in early 2000, the punch line to many business-related jokes features some version of "dot-com." As reported in the January 24, 2000, issue of *Forbes,* "some Net outfits are dropping the dot-com suffix from their company logos, at least in their advertising, to look real. Big Star Entertainment of New York City sells videotapes online and sends them by United Parcel Service. Yet it painted its name (sans dot.com) on 23 local delivery trucks to remind people that it owns some physical assets."

This is also the time when many scheduled dot-com IPOs have been withdrawn and indefinitely delayed due to "adverse market conditions" (read: the public ain't buying). And for good reason. Glance down this list of some of the zoom-to-doom prices of well-known dot-coms:

COMPANY	CLOSE OF FIRST TRADING DAY	RECENT
Chemdex	25.50	3.2
FreeMarkets	280.00	3.7
Neoforma.com	52.38	0.4
PurchasePro.com	17.42	2.7
SciQuest.com	30.00	0.3
VerticalNet	22.69	9.2

A Five-Year History of the Web

1996 **Fewer than one in five large companies have a Web site;** Web page production comes within the reach of average users

1997 **Dramatic rise in Internet Service Providers;** interactive cameras become common on the Internet

1998 **Internet security gains reputation as safe for most transactions;** Java provides new crossover platform tool and becomes an Internet standard

1999 **Most PCs sold with equipment for easy Web access;** Internet business becomes a viable alternative to ordering via toll-free telephone numbers

2000 **Desktop videoconferencing becomes practical and affordable;** one-fourth of all applications (mortgage, job, college, etc.) are processed over the Web; the Internet becomes the central resource for information

PLEASURE AND PAIN

COULD A SIMILAR LIST BE MADE OF DOT-COM SUCCESSES? OF course. But pain apparently resonates longer than pleasure in the investor's mind. We're well past the giddy days where the dot in dot-com suspiciously resembled a cork from a liquor bottle. As Hal Varian, dean of Information Systems at UC-Berkeley, recently wrote, "As the Internet business starts to mature, it will likely consolidate into a market structure with a few big winners (companies like AOL, Yahoo!, Cisco), a few big losers (fill in your candidates here), and lots of perpetually small players focusing on niche markets."

So, here's the message for the heedful in shaky times: Your e-business venture must not merely *seem* real, in its presentation and image on the Internet, but in fact *be* real in the consistent value it offers the customer. Not long ago, investors and consumers were buying the sizzle of e-business, but now they want to see the steak.

Five Great Reasons for Developing a Real E-Business for Real People

IF YOU'RE WILLING TO BUILD A BACK-SHOP BUSINESS OPERA-tion that supports your slick storefront on the Web, you probably already understand the following five reasons for steering your business more and more toward the Internet:

1. The Internet offers a huge potential audience for your service or product.

INTERNET USERS NOW NUMBER MORE THAN 60 MILLION around the world, a number expected to more than double by the end of 2002. What print, radio, billboard, or television promotion approach could serve up such numbers of potential customers? But there's a rub—will some of this vast number turn out to be your customers? According to research by the Gartner Group, less than 1 percent of worldwide Internet users turn out to be consumers, in the sense that they consume anything beyond information by means of the Internet. Nor should you base your business plan on a likely number of "hits" (visits to your Web site) as a percentage of total Web traffic. The total number of site visits, reports SuperStats.com, is skewed significantly by the multimillions of hits each week to the 100,000 or so porn sites now on the Internet. As noted previously, that vast number of hits must be discounted in any sane estimate of business hits on the Web. The same must be said for the average amount of time a person browses on the Web, which was widely quoted for 1999–2000 as 63 minutes per session. When visits to porn sites are subtracted from that average, by some expert estimates it drops by almost half. You should also revise downward the total spending on the Web if you want to subtract the hundreds of millions of dollars spent on the modern-day version of peep shows.

NOT A SOUL CLICKED THROUGH

HERE'S AN INSTRUCTIVE AND CAUTIONARY CASE. INTERNET expert Neil Weinberg tells the story of a small-scale entrepreneur, Donald Azars, who "owns a small video production business called DAPTV Associates and is a self-described klutz when it comes to the dance floor. Recognizing that the world is crowded with the rhythmically challenged, he recently produced a self-instruction video featuring onetime *Lawrence Welk Show* stars Bobby Burgess and Elaine Balden. They promise, 'If you can walk, you can dance.'

"To spread the word, the Los Angeles entrepreneur decided to plug into the Internet. He signed up with BannerExchange.com, one of the legion of services offering small businesses a Web presence on the cheap (free in this case). BannerExchange scattered Azars's Web ad banners among its other clients' Web sites, reserving some of the space for paying customers.

"In Azars's case, not a soul clicked through.... So Azars dropped the service and bought TV infomercial time. Business has poured in since."

Can you imagine the calculations Azars must have made of his potential customer base via the Internet? Let's see, 60 million Internet users, all of whom will have to dance at least once in their lives. If I sell to only one in one thousand, I'll make a fortune! But gross numbers of users do not a customer base make, as Azars learned the hard way.

2. No other medium except face-to-face selling allows the user to "click through" to initiate a purchase or other transaction.

THE BEST MAGAZINE OR NEWSPAPER AD MISSES THE OPPORTUNITY to translate a reader's interest or approval into a "buy" decision. Direct marketing letters also fail in this regard. There's no button to push for direct connection to the company or merchant. Television and radio suffer from a similar disconnect, although interactive TV promises to improve this situation significantly if and when it appears in most households. Although direct telephone marketing potentially allows the message receiver to say "yes" in the form of an immediate order, the almost universal consumer response to this marketing channel is "Why the hell are you calling me at my home—and at dinner time!"

By contrast, a company's own Web page and its advertising on other Web sites contain almost instantaneous access to product or service information. The "yes" decision on the part of the cybershopper is always just a click away. Not that such clicks come inexpensively. When Borders established its Web site in 1998 to compete with Amazon.com and barnesandnoble.com, the popular bookseller spent $5 million (and an estimated $20 million in 1999) in large part for click-through advertising placed on such Internet portals as Yahoo!. The Boston Consulting Group terms such investment "rent," and estimates it can run to 65 percent of sales during the first years when a company is attempting to attract attention and build market share.

3. Barriers to entry are remarkably low, at least at the front-end or Web-visible part of the business.

IN 1997, WEB DEVELOPMENT SERVICES NECESSARY TO GET A smallish company up and running on the Internet were generally quoted in the $3,000 to $5,000 range. By 1998 that estimate had dropped to $2,000 to $2,500. By late 1999, most business magazines guesstimated an investment of $500 to $2,000 for a passably attractive and useful Web site. And by 2000, the cost had dropped to zero, as more than 2,000 Web hosting services offered free help for Web site construction. (Perhaps in the near future Web site developers will outbid one another to pay clients for programming services!)

Free? It's true, and from more than one vendor. Among the newest kids on this most inexpensive of blocks is Bigstep.com. Backed by such firms as Sun Microsystems, the *Washington Post,* and *Newsweek,* this innovative service is designed to get small companies up and running on the Web quickly and for free. The nitty-gritty of the Bigstep.com experience is that after registering, Bigstep lets you create and maintain a site for free, rather than at a monthly rate of up to the $250 that some site-hosting services charge small businesses. If you wish to register a unique Web address or establish merchant credit card services, Bigstep says it passes the associated fees onto customers at cost, with no markup. (The Bigstep business model relies on sponsorships and fees for optional services for revenue.)

An interactive guide walks you through the site creation process using simple, easy-to-understand steps that don't require any previous programming experience. Within minutes, you'll click through menu selections to build a home page and other standard site elements, like a product catalog and a "Contact Us" link. You're not required to complete the process in one sitting, so you can create your site piece by piece in your spare time. When you're done, you'll be part of Bigstep's community of online businesses, rather than being a single site in the vast World Wide Web. Best of all, you'll have risked nothing but your spare time to join the e-business party.

Assistance with more complicated business sites, especially those involving database management, is treated in depth in Step 7—and no, it's hardly free.

Front-end Web site development, whether simple or elaborate, is often misconceived as the major and most important element of business creation. Therein lies the biggest problem with many dot-com businesses: nothing stands behind the Web site. The much-touted "virtual" businesses of the Internet quickly find that they rely on someone's (their own or a partner's) quite physical bricks-and-mortar reality to fulfill customers' orders. In short, the back-shop operation is at least as important as the snazzy Web site for a profitable e-business.

THE CHANGING BUSINESS MODEL AT AMAZON.COM

TAKE THE CASE OF AMAZON.COM. FOUNDED BY JEFF BEZOS in 1994, Amazon was intended to be primarily an electronic storefront, with the heavy lifting of book storage left to Ingram Books, the world's largest book wholesaler. This arrangement allowed Bezos to claim an inventory of 1.1 million titles, although just 500 best-sellers were actually stored in his own 45,000-square-foot facility in Seattle. Over the years, however, Amazon's cozy arrangement with Ingram has slipped, forcing Bezos's firm to store more and more of its own inventory. Consequently, Amazon eventually opened a huge seven-acre warehouse in Nevada, with plans on the books for several more.

This is the "invisible plumbing behind each sale," in the phrase of Kevin Jones, president of Net Market Makers, a business-to-business consulting firm. Amazon must not only advertise discounted prices and quick delivery on a wide range of book titles but also be geared up to deliver on those promises.

4. The future of the Internet is much brighter for business start-ups and entrepreneurial investment than current track records suggest.

AS WE HAVE SEEN, THE INTERNET HAS POSED AT LEAST AS many financial problems as profits for many companies. The allure of what this network of commerce may become, however, remains undeniable. In sheer size of audience, it is still in its infancy. For reasons discussed in Step 8, much of the industrialized world has not yet come aboard. Kevin Kelly of *Wired* magazine puts this rising population of users in a memorable way: "The Internet is actually being underhyped. Of all the people [who will be] online in ten years, only a tenth are online today."

Measured in dollars, the total marketplace represented on the Internet is also expanding robustly. Retail transactions in all forms were estimated to rise to $40 billion by 2002, up dramatically from $8 billion in 1999.

LEVI'S SEEKS A WEB SITE THAT FITS

CATCHING THE WAVE OF THE FUTURE INSTEAD OF TREADING water behind it is crucial to business success. The often-discussed case of Levi Strauss makes the point concretely. Levi's set out to be a front-runner in Internet enterprise by founding its original Web site back in 1994. But for years thereafter the company seemingly refused to paddle to catch the wave. Specifically, it delayed actually selling its clothing over the Internet for fear of alienating its retail dealers. Even when products did become available via the Web site in late 1998, the company withheld its most popular product abroad—its 501 blues—from Internet sales for several more months while it debated pricing policies for Asian and European markets.

In early 1999, all Web advertising and a planned TV campaign for the Web site were abruptly canceled amid Levi's burgeoning financial problems. Between April and September of that year, the sites levi.com and dockers.com failed to attract enough hits to even be noticed by Nielsen NetRatings. In that same period competitors such as Eddie Bauer, Gap, and J. Crew all were listed in the Nielsens. Levi's own major retailers, including J. C. Penney's and Macy's, lobbied hard with Levi's to allow their companies to sell its products over their own Web sites. In what seemed to many a gesture of surrender, Levi's later agreed to such sales and simultaneously pulled the plug on its own Web sales efforts. "We determined that running a first-class e-commerce site was unaffordable," said a press release. It is estimated that Levi's poured $8 million into its ill-fated foray into the Internet.

IF YOU CAN'T BEAT THEM...

ON THE FLIP SIDE, HERE'S A HAPPIER STORY ABOUT RECOGnizing where the market vectors for one's business are pointing. Like many smaller antiques-and-collectibles sellers, Linda Dawson foresaw little good for her twenty-three-year-old family business when the giant auctioneer Sotheby's came onto the Internet. Auction sites on eBay, Yahoo!, and elsewhere had already exposed Dawson's clients to a wide range of antiques at prices far below those she typically charged. It was not uncommon for an in-store customer to delay closing a transaction, Dawson says, until he or she "had checked out comparable prices on the Internet."

She saw, correctly, that the future of her business lay in coming up with a strategy to not only accommodate the Internet but also take advantage of it. "We have to do this to survive," Dawson told her employees.

At the same time, Sotheby's was revising its own Internet strategy. The common wisdom in the antiques business is that selling is the easy part—it's finding the good items to sell that requires hard work and contacts. Sotheby's wisely realized that the greater its auction inventory, the larger the Internet audience it could expect to attract. And in a variation of the chicken-and-egg analogy, the larger the audience clicking onto Sotheby's site, the more sellers would be convinced to place items for auction at Sotheby's.

The auctioneer's strategy was clever. Instead of fighting its competitors, Sotheby's opened its Web site, sothebys.com, to thousands of smaller dealers and auction houses. This big-tent approach gave Sotheby's what it wanted—an exponentially larger inventory to attract client interest. At the same time, member companies such as Dawson's antiques firm got what they wanted—a huge client base considering their items for sale. The arrangement worked as follows: Sotheby's agreed to provide the Web site and handle all billing and collection. Much as on eBay, member companies would appraise, describe, and digitally photograph their wares for presentation on the Web site. They also would be responsible for answering questions from bidders and shipping sold items.

The plan succeeded beyond the expectations of Sotheby's and those of members like Dawson. By its first Web auction under the new strategy, Sotheby's had enrolled 4,660 member companies and expanded its auction inventory to 5,000 lots per week, a fivefold increase from previous inventory levels. At the same time, members were discovering a whole new channel for their businesses. Dawson estimates that e-business accounted for 25 percent of her sales in mid-2000 and that by January 2001 that figure had risen to 50 percent.

A current quick-read business book is entitled *Who Moved My Cheese?* It describes how the future has a nasty habit of moving the "cheese" away from all of us in one way or another. Linda Dawson looked unflinchingly at where her cheese was headed and, through her e-business strategy, followed it courageously and creatively.

5. The Internet remains one of the few economic arenas in which smarts count more than resources. Your hard thinking and careful planning can pay off big.

BY TURNING TO THE INTERNET NOW TO FOUND OR ENHANCE an e-business site, you reap the advantage of others' mistakes. In effect, lessons are all around you on the Web. *Forbes* editorializes that "while tens of thousands of firms are building Web sites, few have any hard plans for using them to do business, and even fewer have any idea just how much such sites cost." To make matters worse, many individuals and companies are playing an expensive and self-deceiving game of Follow the Leader when it comes to Web site development. They fixate on certain companies inside or outside their industry who have ostensibly "done it right." The Web site designs and operations of these companies are then benchmarked as "best practices" and slavishly emulated.

In reality, says Barbara Reilly, research director for the Gartner Group, "when we talk to the companies that others are using as benchmarks, we find that they themselves had no justification for going online; theirs was just an experiment. So what you've got in those cases are a number of different business plans built upon an experiment done by one particular market leader. It's an IT experiment gone haywire."

The result of such confusion in thinking and planning is the current state of affairs on the Web, with thousands of abandoned storefronts ignominiously marking the previous high hopes of their founders. If you click on such a deserted storefront, you may get an "out-of-business" message. But just as often, the Web site facade sits there absolutely abandoned, dead to all clicks. It will eventually be whisked out of cyberspace when the organization hosting the site discovers that its monthly bill isn't being paid.

A GOOD IDEA THAT DIDN'T HAPPEN

LET'S CONSIDER A CASE WHERE GOOD THINKING IN ADVANCE could have saved the financial health of a promising dot-com. Nets Inc. rushed to the Internet with the germ of an attractive business idea: the company would offer a Grand Central Station of electronics product listings drawn from the catalogs of 4,500 member firms, each of which would pay between $1,000 and $200,000 to be listed. At first glance, the business proposition seemed sure to succeed. Wouldn't buyers of electronics in all forms hurry to the Web site for virtually all of their purchases?

As it turned out, no. Notice at least three shortcomings in the initial thinking that went into the site:

- **The Web site simply provided an electronic version of existing catalogs.** Shoppers found no cost savings over their previous purchases from the paper versions of such catalogs. (The lesson: shoppers expect bigger to be cheaper.)
- **The Web site was difficult to use, both for finding comparable items in various catalogs and for performing click-through transactions with dealers.** In effect, shoppers experienced the "no help on the floor" and "not enough checkers" problems familiar from supermarkets.
- **Member electronics companies never grasped what it meant to be part of an "online community" through Nets Inc.** Did it mean that they cut one another special deals? Did it mean that they shared business approaches and secrets? Did it mean that they no longer competed? Their association was never leveraged into anything more than a loosely assembled group of merchants selling similar wares.

Were any of these problems foreseeable from the beginning, especially as the business plan was being forged? Of course. This is a case where more insightful thinking would have saved Nets Inc. and the fortunes of its investors. The company ended up filing for protection from its creditors under federal bankruptcy law.

Summing Up Step 1

AS DESCRIBED IN THIS CHAPTER, THE FIRST STEP ON THE path to e-business success is really a matter of conditioning for the journey. By looking unflinchingly at some of the very real pitfalls of e-business, you are equipping yourself with what Hemingway called "a reliable B.S. detector" (well, he was a bit more vivid). This conditioning process should go on throughout the remaining steps described in this book. Think of your attention to the hard realities and tough-luck stories of e-business as a form of mental calisthenics. You face up to the many unpleasant truths about Internet commerce not to dampen your enthusiasm for your e-business efforts but instead to make sure that your time, energy, and money are well spent.

2

STEP 2

Find Your Unique Place in the E-Business Crowd

NETWORK SOLUTIONS, ONE OF the prominent companies that register site names for the Internet, is now signing up about 10,000 new site names *per week*. Domain names (such as daylesmith.com) are being gobbled up at the rate of more than 1 million per year.

So what? First, you can conclude in advance that you will have competition in some form for the e-business you contemplate. Second, your favorite name for that e-business probably has already been taken. Entire companies such as Greatname.com have been formed around the idea of acquiring thousands of likely names on the cheap, then selling them to start-up e-businesses at premium rates, sometimes in the millions of dollars. Wouldn't you like to be the entrepreneur who originally reserved such names as dogfood.com, fineart.com, pasta.com, paint.com, vacations.com, loans.com, and so forth? Step 7 will help you find a memorable, descriptive name not yet taken by the professional name gluttons. Be assured there's still a place for your creative presence on the crowded e-business scene.

Do You Need to Be Unique?

SURROUNDED BY MILLIONS OF OTHER SITES ON THE Internet, do you really need to strive for your own unique identity? It's a fact that some quite successful e-businesses have positioned themselves as "second-wave" enterprises, content to let the "first-wave" pioneers create the market through expensive advertising and run headlong into the various barriers and problems that may confront the first enterprise in a particular business area. The second-wavers carefully observe the progress of the pioneers, then follow closely behind—but without the missteps made by the first-wavers.

For example, at least fifty e-businesses now focus on selling pre-owned upscale watches, such as Rolex and Cartier. One of the very first such businesses, watches.com, faced a long list of crucial business problems and questions: How can quality used watches be acquired for resale? How do you prevent thieves from fencing stolen watches through your e-business? Can upscale used watches be profitably sold at better prices than those offered by traditional jewelers and watch merchants? What disclosure should be made about the history of a particular watch or some of its weak points (for example, a stretched band or scratched crystal)? What customer guarantees or return policy should be offered, if any? Can upscale watches be sold simply by a photograph?

Often through expensive trial and error, the first-wave merchant struggles through these and other questions. In the background, of course, are many second-wavers taking notes on what works and doesn't work. Therefore, except in cases where business processes or technology are legally protected by copyright or other means, it is a perfectly acceptable strategy to be a "me-too" e-business instead of the trailblazer. No one sued Burger King for making hamburgers that suspiciously resembled those of McDonald's.

Finding What's Special

EVEN IF YOU POSITION YOURSELF AS A FOLLOWER, YOU NEVERtheless will need to search out some characteristics that make your e-business unique. Here are fifteen possible distinguishing features to consider:

1. We offer a wider range of products or services.
2. We offer better-quality products or services.
3. We offer better prices or better terms.
4. We offer an easier ordering process.
5. We offer quicker shipping (order fulfillment).
6. We offer desirable bonuses (such as the vastly successful frequent-flier programs now used by most major airlines).
7. We offer personal attention and service (vs. dealing with a computer program).

8 We stand behind what we sell through reliable guarantees and warranties.
9 We offer connection to a network of services you may need.
10 We offer greater expertise than competitors.
11 We are better known than competitors (and, by implication, are more trustworthy).
12 We have bricks-and-mortar regional facilities where products can be inspected before purchase and returned, if necessary, for warranty work.
13 We offer freebies in the form of "buy two, get one free" promotions.
14 We offer substantial rewards or savings based on how many new customers you refer to our e-business.
15 We have customer satisfaction records that our competitors can't equal.

TAKE A MOMENT RIGHT NOW TO JOT DOWN ANY OF THESE distinguishing features that you plan to emphasize in your e-business. And feel free to think beyond this list—that's what uniqueness is all about.

Your Unique Pricing: Can They Get It for Less Elsewhere?

IN TRADITIONAL CONSUMER BUYING, WE OFTEN PAID TOP dollar because we didn't know any better. We shopped for a Toyota, for example, knowing only that Uncle Al bought a similar one for about $16,000. We felt good when we struck a deal for $15,800. Or we bought a digital camera from a local shop whose prices over the years had always seemed fair to us.

In both these cases, our knowledge base for making purchasing decisions was severely limited. Did we know, for example, the best price for Toyotas in our area (let's say it turns out to be $13,800) or the discount catalog price for the camera we wanted (again, let's say a savings of 40 percent over retail)?

The Internet makes such information readily available to all consumers. (Some companies such as pricescan.com focus exclusively on providing price comparisons on a vast array of products.) Want to buy a trombone for your kid? Certainly you would want to take two minutes to see what trombones of your chosen style and brand are selling for at auction on eBay or Yahoo!. Even if you decide not to take the risk of purchasing by auction, you nevertheless are armed with powerful information the next time you visit your local musical instruments shop: "Six hundred dollars? I saw exactly the same trombone on sale at eBay for $350." That's negotiating leverage!

An Open Market Where Knowledge Is King

THE ALMOST UNIVERSAL AVAILABILITY OF KNOWLEDGE ABOUT best prices must influence how you conceive of your e-business. You probably cannot count on the customer's ignorance of prevailing market conditions for your product to make a high-profit sale. If you are not offering the lowest price (and you may decide not to), there must be powerful compensating factors in your business plan to overcome this point of resistance. New-car sales have had to face up to this truth as more and more buyers come to the showroom completely prepped with information from CarPoint.com, Edmunds.com, and other auto info services telling exactly how much a car of a given model and year should sell for. The auto salesperson has been stripped naked of the old protective armor of secret knowledge. He or she can't con you into paying a higher price once you know the dealer's price for the car as well as the usual markup for that model.

Your e-business, no matter what its products or services, will probably find itself in a similar situation to automobile sales. As much as you would like to charge top dollar for your wares, you will be constrained by the customers' knowledge of what they can get it for elsewhere. That blunt truth has led some Internet analysts to wonder if decent profit margins can be achieved in any retail area, given the buyer's access to perpetual price-cutting by competitors. Scott Blum, founder of Buy.com, despairs of making money from products at all. His current plan is to sell some products below cost in hopes of building a large enough audience to attract lucrative advertising.

Speaking of e-business retailing, Blum concludes that "this is just a catalog retailing business with lower barriers to entry. Margins, if they ever materialize, will always be crummy." As a sign of the times, in March 2000 mighty Dell Computer announced that it would move away from online sales of its wide range of PCs. The market has been so undercut by lowball competitors that Dell cannot sustain a profitable margin on the computers it sells.

CAN YOU BE SPECIAL ENOUGH TO DEMAND TOP DOLLAR?

IT'S A BIT OF A TRICK, BUT PERHAPS YOU CAN BE SPECIAL ENOUGH to demand top dollar in your e-business. That "special" quality can be achieved in any number of ways, including your name recognition, delivery efficiency, range of products, or bonus attractions. Here are several "beyond price" techniques now being used successfully by e-business companies:

- **Amazon.com undeniably charges higher prices than most of its competitors, yet it remains the most popular shopping destination on the Internet (and not just for books).** This sustained popularity has surprised economists who thought that price ruled all. University of Maryland economist Joseph Bailey notes, "A couple years ago, economists were predicting that the transparency of the Internet [being able to see and compare all prices at all times] would lead to a price war that would kill profits. Now people are beginning to ask if the Internet is breeding natural monopolies."

  It was supposed to work quite differently, economists point out. Consumers should be drawn like flies to the vendor with the lowest price. Companies that couldn't compete would disappear, leaving the market with the "low-price leaders" (in the jargon of economists, narrow price dispersion for similar products).

  But here's the surprise that Amazon and others have enjoyed: once a consumer has a pleasing, no-hassle buying

Profit Squeeze

E-TAILERS HAVE LITTLE ROOM for profit even if marketing costs and rent fall, as shown below.

	SUPERSTORES	ONLINE
AVERAGE SALE	$100.00	$100.00
DISCOUNT	10.00	20.00
SHIPPING & HANDLING	-	11.00
SALES TAX	7.00	-
CUSTOMER PAYS	97.00	91.00
COST OF SALES	67.41	57.60
SHIPPING & HANDLING	2.88	9.90
GROSS PROFIT	26.71	23.50
OPERATING EXPENSES		
RENT	0.96	4.55
LABOR & STORE	10.75	-
WEB SITE DEVELOPMENT		2.90
MARKETING	2.50	17.29
TOTAL	14.21	24.74
OPERATING PROFIT PER ORDER	12.50	-1.24

SOURCE: CHRISTOPHER VROOM, THOMAS WEITZEL PARTNERS

experience with an online merchant such as Amazon, the customer tends to be less price sensitive in doing business again with that merchant, especially if the price difference is only a few bucks. (Interestingly, a group of researchers at Pennsylvania State University has developed compelling evidence that online shoppers may quickly become less price sensitive than when they are shopping in the bricks-and-mortar world of Sears, Macy's, or Home Depot.)

Here's an example of the price bonus Amazon is achieving through its customer loyalty. In 2000, an Olympus D450 digital camera could be purchased for $397.98 on Onvia.com but sold like hotcakes through Amazon at $499.99.

- **Charles Schwab & Co. continues to charge more per trade than most of its competitors (for example, many stock trades costing more than $100 at Schwab contin-**

ue to cost only $12 at TDWaterhouse and other discount brokers). Through a remarkable and intensive advertising campaign, Schwab has attempted to instill its name in clients' minds as the symbol and proof of superior service, reliability, and access to investment resources. To date the strategy has worked. Clients will ruefully admit that they pay Schwab more than they should but point to a long relationship with the famed broker and the ease of reaching individuals within the Schwab organization as justification for the higher brokerage fees.

- **UPS has a strategy of getting a foot inside the door of a potential client, then embedding UPS services so thoroughly in the client's business processes that a divorce becomes unlikely.** For example, if you enter an order through the Web site of Micron Electronics, your message will in fact be sent directly to UPS. The shipper assigns a tracking number to your order and, after checking Micron's inventory, informs you by e-mail (in the name of Micron) when your order will be delivered. In the works are UPS-generated e-mails (again, ostensibly from Micron) informing you when a shipment is delayed or back ordered. What Micron reaps from such an arrangement, of course, is huge cost savings in not having to process its own order stream. But what UPS gains is perhaps more revolutionary: Micron as a long-term client not because UPS has the best prices or service but because it has inextricably inserted itself into the business processes of Micron, its client.

On a smaller scale, mom-and-pop shops on the Internet can often achieve quite respectable profit margins by being at the right place at the right time. The chiefs at Yahoo!, Lycos, Excite, InfoSeek, AOL, and other search services are looking to just these small players to become the real Internet successes of the decade.

In its current development, the commercial sector of the Internet seems to be emerging as a vast array of relatively small niche marketers, each attuned to the specific needs of highly localized markets. Such a business environment is ideal for the small operator with expertise, let's say, in collectible plates, quality used musical instruments, difficult-to-locate auto parts, or customized services such as writing or editing assistance. These are not "off-the-shelf" products or services that can easily be offered by a major retailer such as Wal-Mart.

Visiting the Mall

IN THEIR ORIGINAL BUSINESS PLANS, THE GIANT SEARCH engines thought that advertising would be their ever-growing cash cow as more and more people came to their search sites. But as detailed in Step 8, Internet advertising rates for banner ads have plummeted in the past year as we all discovered together that an Internet ad just doesn't have the pulling or branding power of a TV or print ad. At worst, banners and pop-up ads are insectlike annoyances to be clicked away as quickly as possible. We wish we could swat them permanently.

Robert Davis, CEO of Lycos, says, "We aren't losing faith in advertising, but it isn't growing as quickly as commerce. The selling opportunity ahead of us is overwhelming." Similarly at InfoSeek, says CEO Harry Motro, "online retailing is our fastest-growing segment—by a very large margin."

These 800-pound gorillas in the Internet world are turning to the creation of electronic malls populated by good-value (but not necessarily lowest-price) shops of all kinds. The search company skims off a percent of sales and often profits as well from "enrollment and setup" fees to merchants. The goal here is to direct the hundreds of thousands of site visitors to the main sites (Amazon.com, Yahoo.com, and so on) to an associated mall for pleasurable shopping. "The mission here is the consumer," says America Online's president, Robert Pittman. "The online shopping world is just like the physical world of shopping. What matters is location, location, location—and that's what we give people."

Echoes Barbara Reilly, research director of the Gartner Group, "We're not going to see mass markets—the equivalent of cyber Wal-Mart or cyber Home Depot. The key to understanding electronic commerce over the Internet is to think of it as a lot of little malls, with a lot of little stores. And the challenge is going to be getting the customers to where you are."

THE RIGHT PLACE AT THE RIGHT TIME

THAT PERSPECTIVE MUST OFFER GOOD NEWS TO SMALL BUSINESSES who knew in advance they could not compete in scope or scale with the Staples, Lands' End, and Amazons of the world. What they can be, however, is Johnny-on-the-spot when a consumer is visiting his or her mall. MyCandies.com can be an impulse click by a customer scanning the little shops made available through the AOL Mall, Yahoo! Mall, or other big services. If the candy is attractively displayed and made easy to purchase (with easy click processing, Visa and MasterCard options, and similar conveniences), the consumer may well spend money at the site without checking out the prices six ways from Sunday. In short, there are times we all accept somewhat higher prices when we believe we are getting good product in a timely, pleasurable way and without hassle. The last time you strolled down the quaint street of a tourist town, you paid too much for fudge. That candy store was at the right place at the right time to persuade you to fork over $5 for a little square of heaven.

THE HOLY GRAIL OF RETAILING: 'I'M THE ONLY PLACE YOU CAN BUY...'

PERHAPS YOU HAVE A RETAILING IDEA SO UNIQUE THAT there's nothing like it on the Internet. If so, *shhh*—loose lips sink ships. Let's say, for purposes of illustration, that you've acquired Internet distribution rights to a universal gas cap to replace all those auto gas caps lost in service stations, on the freeway, and elsewhere. Best of all, you can sell the cap profitably for 25 percent less than any competing cap in auto parts stores or dealers' showrooms. It packs easily and ships cheaply. You have all the ingredients for e-business success—except customers.

You hope to advertise your unique product by a fitting domain name. Alas, your favorite choices—gascap.com, lostyourcap.com, getacap.com, and cheapcap.com—are all reserved by others. So you settle for something that doesn't exactly roll off the tongue but at least captures your business idea: replacementgascaps.com.

At this point your uniqueness becomes your curse as well as your blessing. You can't check out the several sites of your competitors to see how they are attracting customers, because these sites don't exist. You don't fit the mall profile for inclusion in minimalls developed by search companies and ISPs because you have just a single product, albeit a good one. You devote $10,000 to an advertising experiment and place eye-catching banner ads on several of the large auto sales and auto auction sites (in the belief that people interested in cars may also have at least one car with a missing gas cap). When a customer clicks on your banner ad, he or she is taken directly to your Web site, where the full story of your universal cap is told and an opportunity to buy is presented.

The economics here are worth telling. Yahoo! promised you that your banner ad would be exposed, however briefly, to 300,000 viewers over a one-month period. That's a CPM (cost per thousand viewers) of about $30, very much in line with rates charged by regional television, newspapers, and auto magazines. So you invested your $10,000 in banner ads and sat back to wait for business to explode.

It never did. You got a total of five hits from the banner ad during the month it ran. Two hits came from people who apparently thought you were selling headwear—they e-mailed you their head sizes. Two hits came from gas-cap manufacturers who wanted to sell you product. And one hit came from a bona fide customer—but he drove a truck and your caps don't fit trucks.

When Banners Go Bust

HAVING AN EXPERIENCE WITH WEB-BASED ADVERTISING LIKE the one described above is not unusual. More than 80 percent of all Web ad space goes unsold on any given day, even at magnet sites like Yahoo! and AOL. Commissions to agencies who place Internet ads can be outrageously high—30 to

70 percent—versus the commission for placing print or media ads, which rarely exceeds 15 percent. And it's a case of feast or famine for the Web sites themselves: the twenty-five sites receiving the most traffic get about 80 percent of all advertising spending, while the hundreds of thousands of lesser sites seeking ads get the crumbs or nothing at all.

The return on investment in advertising has always been difficult to track and measure. But by consensus among e-business sites on the Internet, advertising rarely justifies its current expense. As noted earlier, big search companies such as Yahoo! and Lycos are looking beyond advertising revenues to commissions on retail sales as their primary earning channel. Many companies find that expenditures on advertising exceed the gross sales that were supposed to arise from those ads.

As a consequence, prices for Web advertising have fallen through the floor and will soon reach the basement. According to Beth Haggerty, senior vice president at InfoSeek, most search companies will quote advertising prices in the $8 to $10 per CPM range—but will also negotiate downward from there if times are lean.

How is it possible that 300,000 people glanced at a banner ad for replacement gas caps and almost none clicked through to purchase one? Consider your own response to banner ads that appear on your screen. Do you read them at all? Do you give consideration to buying by clicking on the ad? If so, how many ads do you give such serious consideration? One in 10? One in 100? One in 1,000? Perhaps your own experience with Internet ads can explain better than any theory of perception or motivation how hundreds of thousands of people can see but not really take notice of a banner ad that flits in the way of their work and then flits or is clicked away.

As we shall see in Step 8, you can experiment with banner advertising without spending money. You can also use the many other techniques described in that step to market your e-business, all of them potentially more promising than banner ads.

Summing Up Step 2

WITH HUNDREDS OF THOUSANDS OF COMMERCIAL WEB SITES now on the Internet and thousands more pouring in each week, few Web site entrepreneurs can claim to be completely unique in what they offer or how they run their e-businesses. But you can develop your own special edge amid such competition—perhaps your competitive advantage in pricing, customer service, product range and availability, regional focus, marketing power, or management efficiency. Finding that "special something" in your e-business is crucial to its success.

3

STEP 3

Shape Your E-Business Idea

IT'S NOW TIME TO THINK FREELY AND SPECULatively about your e-business concept. Don't cast anything in concrete, and for heaven's sake, don't sign any development or site hosting contracts yet. This should be a period of days, or sometimes weeks, in which you think through your concept from at least four perspectives: (1) the customer's point of view; (2) the owner's (your own) point of view; (3) a competitor's point of view; and (4) an employee's point of view. This approach to shaping your e-business idea applies equally well to entrepreneurs establishing their own firms or corporate employees founding or enhancing an e-business site for their companies.

To begin shaping a successful e-business concept, let's work through three e-business concepts of increasingly larger proportions. The first is a single-owner shop in one of the many malls growing up at present on the Internet. The second is a bit more complicated: an "infomediary" dot-com for the equipment rental industry. The third, and largest in terms of capital investment in equipment and factory space, is a custom fabrication operation for sleeping bags. The company solicits contracts for its products and sells a broad range of sleeping bags via the Internet.

The purpose of walking through the shaping of each of these ideas is to demonstrate in a concrete way the range of hows, whats, wheres, whys, and what-ifs you should be asking about your own e-business concept. (If you've arrived at this page in the book without an e-business idea, these three very different projects may suggest directions for you to pursue in developing your own concept.)

The Small E-Business Project: A Mom-and-Pop Shop

IF ON YOUR WAY TO WORK YOU HAVE LOOKED LONGINGLY AT a nicely appointed art gallery, a busy specialty-foods store, or a boutique clothing store and thought, "I could do that!" the door is wide open to start such a business on the Internet without quitting your day job. As noted previously, major search companies and Internet service providers (ISPs) are presently revising their business models to include "merchant communities" and "online malls" made up of just the kinds of shops listed above.

Here's a specific example of how one such arrangement works. Bellsouth, Mindspring, and other prominent ISPs will help you find a place within one of their malls (actually, an advertised menu of shopping possibilities presented by the ISP as part of its home page). To help you turn looky-lous into buyers, these ISPs may well turn you on to Intershop Communications software. This company, with bases in San Francisco and Hamburg, Germany, has produced innovative software that now runs 40,000 shops and storefronts on the Web, including those for Harrods, Celestial Seasonings, and Electronic Arts.

The special wrinkle in Intershop software is that it makes virtually every aspect of your Web page a selling opportunity. Let's say that you want to open a clothing boutique. On your opening Web page appear three models dressed in some of your most popular items. Like what you see? If so, the customer has simply to click on any item of dress (the models aren't for sale) and be transported directly to a display page with full information about the garment and how to order it. Says one owner of such a boutique, "I've sold my tie more than a thousand times. When I put my image on my opening Web page, I didn't consciously think about selling what I was wearing. But people keep clicking on the tie, which in fact is one of the items we sell. And now it's one of our most popular items, thanks to the Intershop software we use."

While we're enjoying the boutique atmosphere, here's one unique service that may be useful both in creating and in maintaining your chosen type of shop. Founded in 1999 by Kris Hagerman, Affinia (www.affinia.com) is a free Web service that allows entrepreneurs to create their own online stores. The product mix can be anything you choose, made all the easier by the 1,000 online merchants Hagerman has assembled for your use. Many have package purchase plans that you let stock your shop inexpensively at the beginning, then build a deeper and more varied inventory as business grows. One woman restricted her shop's offerings to Hummel ceramics. By buying wholesale in quantity and selling at retail below the cost of Hummels in gift stores, she has attracted a loyal, steady clientele. In 1999 she reported gross revenues of more than $1 million.

A similar success story, though more of a rags-to-riches tale, is that of a Southern California gardener who in his spare time made old-fashioned one-piece rolling pins on his wood lathe. Instead of setting up a shop per se, he decided to use the proven marketing pull of eBay and Yahoo! auctions to see if his rolling pins would sell. Fearing that he would be stuck with boxes of rolling pins in his living room, he put the whole lot of 100 up for sale at auction on eBay. To his delight, they sold to a prominent antiques and collectibles dealer for $720. "It took me about three days to make those rolling pins," the now-former gardener says, "and about $30 in materials. I've been doing it now for six months and have brought in a total of $42,000. I'm planning to hit six figures in my first year. Then I will probably bring in some employees and step up production considerably." A star is born!

Early in 2000 Prodigy set in motion an aggressive and expensive advertising campaign to attract small businesses to its range of services. Prodigy's offerings for small business are laid out in three packages: Starter Class, Business Class, and Enterprise Class. Let's say our Mom and Pop opt for a shop in the Starter Class category. For $50 per month, Prodigy will host their site containing up to fifty products; in addition, the folks pay 80¢ for every e-transaction above

$100. As their business grows, they may want to step up to Business Class for $80, with a limit of 100 products shown on the Web site, or $250 for Enterprise Class, with 1,000 products allowed.

DEPENDING ON YOUR POINT OF VIEW

LET'S CONCLUDE THIS ANALYSIS OF THE RELATIVELY SMALL e-business project by examining it from the four perspectives suggested at the beginning of the chapter. From the point of view of the customer, the e-shop we have begun to shape plays well so long as it (1) stocks my favorites at prices I consider reasonable, (2) tempts me on an ongoing basis with new items in line with my purchasing habits, and (3) delivers my purchases promptly, with quick, gracious resolution of any problems. Your goal as a shop owner should be to track and manage these three aspects of customer service.

From the owner's point of view, the entire system should be easy to manage. Sales should connect directly to inventory and purchasing. Frequent reports should be available to show consumer trends, back-ordered items, financial data, and so forth. In most cases, the owner should attempt to get out of the warehousing and shipping aspects of the business (both labor intensive and expensive) and concentrate instead on managing information, strategy, and relationships.

From the competitor's point of view, I should find it difficult to pierce the "knowledge armor" surrounding your business secrets. It should not be easy to discover where you get your stock, how much you pay, how you contact or correspond with customers, or how your business is progressing. To a competitor who doesn't have your client base or attractive product offerings, it should remain a perpetual mystery "how in the heck they do it!" Even if competitors can successfully imitate some aspect of your e-business, they should never be able to duplicate the whole package of your services.

The view from an employee's perspective should be one of constant, pleasurable challenges, marked by frequent celebrations of progress and recognition of hard work. Few employees labor away just for the satisfaction of seeing the computer screen flicker or the clock tick toward lunch hour. Make every effort to humanize your e-business experience for your employees (much in the way that webvan.com hires delivery people who enjoy being of service to others). A good way to begin lies in reminding employees that behind each e-business transaction are real people who look forward to future dealing with the company if their initial experiences are happy ones.

An excellent place to begin your development efforts is at the Better Business Bureau's online resources, www.bbbonline.com. In particular, look carefully at the bureau's suggested Code of Online Business Practices as you shape a credible e-business. Russ Bodoff, senior vice president and CEO of the BBB, points out that "traditional cues don't exist on the Net, so you have to build levels of trust that help with customer satisfaction, which is critical for Web success."

The Medium-Sized E-Business Project: An 'Infomediary' Niche

LET'S SAY YOU HAVE A LARGER IDEA IN MIND, ONE THAT potentially involves thousands of customers throughout North America and eventually around the world. You plan to position your company as an "infomediary"—a firm that gathers and distributes information to the advantage of the member companies. Your idea goes like this: You know the multibillion-dollar equipment rental business well (everything from tractors to floor polishers to party supplies) and recognize a central problem plaguing that industry. Because most equipment rental companies are independently owned and to some degree compete against one another in their regions, there has traditionally been little communication or "horse-trading" among owners of separate companies. Expensive equipment sits idle at Company A that would be just what Company B would like to have, and vice versa. Too often, Company B goes out and buys the desired piece of equipment for full market price, while Company A sells the same idle piece of equipment for 10¢ on the dollar to a customer or contractor.

BUSINESS-TO-BUSINESS TRANSACTION FUNDAMENTALS

YOU WANT TO CREATE A WIN-WIN ELECTRONIC TRADING floor where owners of equipment rental companies can list what they want to acquire and also list what they want to dispose of. One person's trash will forever be another person's treasure, you reason. Owners have everything to gain from such an arrangement. You believe you can fairly charge an ongoing subscription fee to owners for membership in your network. You can also charge about 5 percent of the total value of any transaction for your role in expediting paperwork. The parties themselves will handle pickup and delivery. You are not involved in warranting the condition of any of the equipment traded. That's a matter of "buyer beware" and is entirely up to the parties themselves. You know that these men and women are quite savvy, however, when it comes to appraising the shape of equipment—they do it every day when equipment returns from a client to their rental yard—and so do not anticipate problems from cheated or disappointed members.

Unlike the mom-and-pop shop described earlier, you are involved in B2B (business-to-business) transactions. To help shape your idea, you look around to see how comparable infomediaries have plied their trade in other industries. One that strikes your interest is Neoforma, based in Santa Clara, California. This company makes nothing and sells nothing to the public. Instead, its mission is to bring health care equipment buyers and sellers together over the Internet. The transactions that take place between these parties can include anything from X-ray machines to bedpans and disposable syringes. The company's infomediary Web site, neoforma.com, gets more than 100,000 hits from viewers each week, half of which come from international sources. On any given day, more than 100,000 items are available for sale (or, in some cases, for donation to charitable medical organizations).

A similar infomediary with a different audience is Intelisys Electronic Commerce. In October 1999, this company inked a deal with Intuit, the software giant famous for management and accounting software, in which Intuit agreed to link the 2.8 million small-business users of its QuickBook programs directly to Intelisys's network of 600 suppliers of business products of all kinds. Intelisys's role as the infomediary is to bring together buyers from many industries to purchase everything from office supplies to air-conditioning filters and bed linens at attractive "membership" prices. Intelisys provides software to automate the purchase-approval process, making it far easier for members to buy from within the network than to go outside to another vendor.

One happy customer is Western Geophysical, which adopted the Intelisys system in June 1999. It uses the Intelisys network of suppliers for 60 percent of the $200 million it spends each year on operating supplies, repair, and maintenance for its seismic surveying business. The time it takes for the company to get approval and order replacement parts for air conditioners and other equipment has been cut from ten days to as little as two minutes using the Intelisys online system.

But back to your dream. In seeking to unite rental equipment companies under one big tent, you know that achieving critical mass will be crucial to the success of your plan. Once a core group of companies start enjoying the benefits of their Internet link, it will be easy for you to attract new members. But how to begin? That question is typical of the crucial issues you must face in shaping your e-business idea. The shallow thing to do, of course, is to avoid the question altogether under the assumption that if you build it, they will come. EuroDisney surely made that mistake during its early years in France. Key to your determination of whether to proceed with your infomediary is the matter of gaining a threshold level of original members. Also key to your success will be demonstrating to those early members that the system is indeed useful. It's a classic chicken-and-egg problem: members will come to your door once they see the value of the Web site, but the Web site cannot demonstrate its true value until members come to your door.

Our function in this chapter is not to solve these core

problems but instead to use them as a way of pointing out the importance of mulling over your e-business idea as thoroughly and insightfully as possible. A sticky problem faced and solved at the shaping stage can avert the financial disaster that would result if the problem were discovered too late in the business rollout.

The Large-Scale E-Business Project: A Manufacturing Operation

IN OUR PREVIOUS TWO EXAMPLES, THE ENTREPRENEURS involved had no hands-on relationship with the products and services they sold. They were middlemen to the transactions. In this final, large-scale example, let's assume that you have the technical and manufacturing expertise to produce a product of some kind and the resources to permit you to gear up for the manufacturing process. Furthermore, you've chosen the Internet as your primary distribution channel in order to avoid the profit-robbing cut taken by traditional retail middlemen. You feel that you can sell high-quality products directly to the public at prices far below typical retail prices.

To put a face on this example, let's put you in the sleeping-bag business. With the resurgence of public attraction toward healthful outdoor living and vacationing, you feel there is a rising market for high-quality sleeping bags. Your competitive advantage, you feel, is that you produce bags in a variety of body sizes. Dad no longer has to wriggle into a sleeping bag that is designed for little Suzy. People can choose their own sizes, much as they do with clothes.

Producing such bags is no problem for you. You've been in the business for years and have all the necessary arrangements made for suppliers of raw materials, a suitable fabrication facility, a trained workforce, and solid management. Your one unknown is how to get your product line successfully to market. Previously you advertised directly to buyers at sports and department stores through catalogs and personal visits by traveling sales personnel. But this Internet thing is a whole new challenge for you.

Should you try to attract public attention to a catchy domain name, such as sleepingbags.com? You investigate this option and are appalled at the kind of advertising budget it would probably take to plant your company's name, product, and Web site name in the public mind.

GOING WHERE CUSTOMERS ARE "FOR SALE"

YOUR INSTINCTS TELL YOU TO GO WHERE THE TRAFFIC already is rather than trying to bring it down the block to your place of electronic business. Amazon.com, for example, boasts a clientele of 12 million customers. Thanks to a new business development at Amazon in late 1999, those customers are "for sale" to merchants and manufacturers like you who have a warehouse of product to move. You investigate and discover the new Amazon zShops program works like this: You must pay Amazon $10 a month and a commission ranging from 1.25 percent to 5 percent. The 12 million Amazon customers are given the opportunity on the Amazon home page to type in key words for what they want to buy. When they type in "sleepingbag," for example, up pops not the 14,506 references to "sleepingbag" that might be found through a typical search engine but instead—to your delight—just your Web site, with complete product pictures and descriptions. The shopper can simply click and buy. You, rather than Amazon, are responsible for shipping and handling. Amazon will handle credit card transactions for an extra 60¢ and 4.75 percent of the sale.

You do some quick calculations based on the assumption that virtually all of your customers will buy by credit card over the Internet. If Amazon is able to sell 100 sleeping bags at an average price of $100 in a month, that's a gross of $10,000, of which Amazon keeps about $1,000, or 10 percent, for its part of the deal. You compare that result with your former sales through retail channels; there, middlemen ended up taking about 50 percent of the eventual retail price. You would have netted only about $5,000 under the old arrangement versus $9,000 under the Amazon plan. You're also free under this arrangement to explore other marketing channels for your products. Amazon doesn't own you.

Thinking through the Basic Purposes of Your E-Business Concept

YOU'RE UNDERSTANDABLY EAGER TO UNVEIL YOUR WEB SITE to the world. But before spending time or money on its development (explained fully in Step 7), take a moment at this shaping stage to decide what it is that you want your Web site to accomplish.

According to the Gartner Group, the biggest mistake entrepreneurs and companies make is thinking about the Web site as "a repository for stale, static corporate publications." According to Gartner vice president Doug Cayne, "CIOs who say, 'We should put our press releases, annual reports, and marketing literature on the Web,' might as well add, 'And maybe someone, somewhere, will actually read them.'"

Cayne lists five core functions a well-thought-out Web site can perform:

1 **Purchase motivator.** Web sites at their best can be a motivating experience that leads consumers through the product information stage to and beyond the buying decision.

2 **Problem solver.** Companies within and across industries can use consumer information and product data available on the Internet to address and resolve business problems. Sound business planning can also make use of these information resources.

3 **Disintermediation.** This is a fancy word for a commonsense idea: sell directly to the eventual customer without going through a middleman. By keeping control over its service relations with customers, companies can build loyalty and avoid apologizing for an intermediary's mistakes.

4 **Information delivery.** The type and timing of information delivered to company stakeholders has long been a key element in business success. A Web site, well used, allows a company to customize and time both "print" information and visual/auditory presentations for distinct stakeholder audiences. What an analyst has access to, using a password, may be quite different from what a first-time customer sees at the Web site.

5 **Customer/vendor communication.** The Web site can become the electronic suggestion box and feedback repository for customers and vendors who want to tell the company something important, pro or con, about its products or services. The old gripe about traditional suggestion boxes, of course, is that they were never emptied on the president's desk to be read. The same fate can befall Web site feedback channels if they are not monitored carefully and responded to in a timely way. As an experiment, one business-magazine editor used the feedback addresses on the Web sites of eight major companies to send a simple message: "Please tell me the name and e-mail address of your CEO." In a majority of cases, the editor received no response at all from the companies. One company, Coca-Cola, responded only several weeks after receiving the request.

TWO HIGHLY SUCCESSFUL LARGE-SCALE WEB SITES THAT MAKE good use of the principles described above are Federal Express and Goodyear. Both committed at an early stage of Web planning to make their sites useful to customers—in effect, these companies wanted customers to come to their sites for a reason, not as a favor. The Federal Express Web site (fedex.com) allows customers anywhere in the world to track shipments by keying in a tracking number from their shipping bills. The company has saved millions of dollars in reduced staffing costs and 800-number charges, both of which were previously necessary to handle these customer inquiries. From the customer's point of view, the system saves time and effort. It's no longer necessary to wait in a phone queue to be served or to repeat long numbers more than once to the operator.

Goodyear, too, focused a portion of its Web site directly on its customers' needs. After discovering that most tire customers don't know what size tires their car should have or what alternate sizes they can consider, Goodyear installed Tire Selector at its Web site (goodyear.com). Consumers can enter the year and model of their car, along with information about the weather in their area and their typical driving habits, and receive by almost immediate e-mail a list of the most suitable Goodyear tires for their specifications. The next interface for the system will no doubt be a telephone number or e-mail address for locations where the customer can have the recommended tires installed. A bonus coupon of some type would also be a motivating touch.

Summing Up Step 3

NO WEB SITE CAN BE ALL THINGS TO ALL PEOPLE. TO ATTEMPT to do so is to ensure failure. From the outset, assess what you hope your Web site to accomplish. Will it be a sales portal where customers can be led smoothly through the buying process? A problem-resolution site where customers can find expert suggestions for fixing, expanding, or upgrading products? A customer-direct site that cuts out the middleman? An information source about the company for stakeholders and the general public? A customer relations site where feedback can be registered and responded to? Knowing the e-business target you hope to hit is obviously paramount in importance in deciding what business arrows to shoot and where to aim them.

4

STEP 4

Investigate Your E-Business Competition

THE OLD SAW ABOUT "THOSE WHO DON'T KNOW history are doomed to repeat it" is especially true of new start-ups in e-business. You don't have to stumble where your competitors have—if you spend time investigating their approaches to the business. Below are ten suggestions for getting to know your competitors better than they may know themselves.

Ten Ways to Get to Know Your Competitors

1 **Get out your notepad or open your computer note-taking program.** You will probably be looking at many competitors or similar companies. Your goal in this "due diligence" exercise should be to map out the entire lay of the land in your field, as best you can discover it, before blazing your own trail in e-business.

2 **Use several search engines (Yahoo!, AOL, Lycos, InfoSeek, AltaVista, MSN, and Netscape would**

make a good start) to see what key words from your business turn up. You will be surprised, first, that different search engines yield such different results. Second, you may be surprised (appalled?) by the incredible number of people doing e-business in your field. A friend considering an e-business in signed lithographs was recently amazed to find 720 direct competitors within a fifteen-minute search time. He claims that he easily could have found 1,000 more if he had worked on the search for another hour.

3 **Select likely competitors from your search and print out their contact information from the search screen.** (There will be time later to go to their home pages on a spy mission.)

4 **Now seek out associations or trade organizations that may list companies doing business in your area.** Many of these companies may not have Web sites,

but that does not mean you cannot learn from their approaches to the business. Add the companies you find to your master list, along with any identifying or clarifying information you discover. At this point, let's assume that you have several dozen companies on your master list.

5 **Prioritize your investigation according to the apparent success of each of the Web sites you plan to visit.** In some cases, this success will be self-proclaimed ("We are the leading supplier of..."), or it may be inferred from the counter at the bottom of the home page, showing how many visitors have viewed the page within a particular time period. You can also use common sense in putting recognizable names toward the top of your list. If you've heard of the company, there's a good chance it is a major player in your field.

6 **Before you begin your intensive investigation of the top ten or so competitors on your list, spend some time at PriceScan or Esmart (pricescan.com, esmart.com).** These services gather pricing data for a vast array of product lines and show who's selling what at the high, middle, and low ends. Their mission, simply put, is to put buying control back in the hands of consumers. "Big vendors can't get away with charging higher prices just because customers don't know any better," says David Cost, CEO of PriceScan. His site attracts 9,000 visitors a day at present and is growing rapidly. Compare your projected product prices to what you find at these transparency sites (so called because they make pricing transparent instead of opaque to the consumer). In this way, you will be seeing your pricing just as your customer will see it. If you're not at or near the low end, you will have to develop strategies to attract and hold customers without appealing to the price advantage. Note the names of competitors that appear on these comparison lists.

7 **Now it is time for some heavy lifting. You're going to visit ten or more competitive Web sites.** When possible, you're going to send e-mail questions about product information, pricing policies (discounts, and so on), payment options, and anything else you would like to learn about with an eye toward developing your own successful e-business. If the company publishes an annual report, obtain one at your

library or, more likely, through your stockbroker. For truly interesting competitors, you may want to spend a few bucks to order one of their products. See how the transaction is handled. You may want to send the product back to evaluate their customer service. Again, keep careful notes on what you discover about each of the companies you investigate.

8 **Armed with what by now may be sheaves of information about competitive companies, reduce your notes to three columns:**

BEST PRACTICES	COMMON PRACTICES	BAD PRACTICES

Under the "Best Practices" column, jot down the business features that truly impressed you about a competitor's operations, Web site, customer relations, or other matters. What "come-ons" or other motivators do they employ? These are the practices you will want to meet and exceed in developing your e-business.

Next, jot down practices that seem to be common across many competitors. Do they all accept more credit cards than the standard Visa and MasterCard? Are they usually members of a credit card service such as PayPal? Do they typically offer money-back guarantees to assure customer satisfaction? What time period do they usually estimate for delivery? These will be the practices that will require important decisions from you: which do you want to follow, and which do you want to ignore or alter?

In the last column, jot down practices that appall you. These can range from click buttons that just don't work on the competitor's Web site, deceptive or incomplete product information, the absence of any human name or feedback e-mail address on the Web site, and anything else that strikes you as poor business practice. These will be the practices that you will avoid—and teach your employees to avoid.

9 **Now make an effort to judge the success of your primary competitors.** If they are publicly traded, check out their stock prices over a period of time and obtain (and read!) reports on the companies prepared by investment analysts.

If such information is not available, write, call, or e-mail the company to request more information. You will be surprised how many firms will be happy to mail you their complete press (or PR) kit, which usually contains more than you would ever want to know about their products and operations. Or the company may send you a potential-investor's kit, especially if they are still making the rounds for venture capital funding. In all these ways, you can peek inside the operations of some of your competitors to learn from their ups and downs.

10 **Finally, condense all your work into a document of no more than two pages.** Title this document something like "Analysis of My Competition." On these two pages, put down the ideas and observations that have impressed you the most during your investigation. These insights will be extremely important as you turn to the next step toward e-business success: formalizing and conceptually testing your business idea.

IN ANALYZING THE OPERATIONS OF COMPETITORS, YOU MAY discover (as many e-business entrepreneurs have) that you need to think of e-business in very different terms than you used for thinking about traditional bricks-and-mortar operations. This is especially true in cases where "back-shop" activities are involved. In a traditional store, the back shop is devoted to receiving large shipments of goods and then, after inventory control, placing them out for customer purchase. In the world of e-business, the back shop usually must be converted significantly to a packing-and-wrapping operation, where small orders are prepared for shipment to thousands of individual customers.

Borders, for example, was ill-prepared for this drastic shift in day-to-day back-shop activities when the company opened its Web site in May 1999. One journalist described Borders CEO Philip Pfeiffer as a "reluctant cybernaut" for the tone and content of Pfeiffer's statement at the Web opening: "Books, music, and video have all been substantially discounted. Consumers get good value, but in the long run margins are inadequate to support the business regardless of how much volume is done." Borders steeled itself to face a loss of $10 million from its Web operation in 1999 and an additional $20 million in 2000. Best practices these are not!

Watching for Special Situations and Turmoil in Your Competition

CHINKS IN THE ARMOR OF COMPETITORS CAN BE OBSERVED by their willingness to provide "desperate measures" to allay customer anger. At Shopping.com, for example, the company's cybersystem just wasn't up to the task of servicing the Christmas rush of customers, many of whom wanted to talk to a real human being to have their questions answered about products, delivery time, credit options, and so forth. Customers were complaining to all who would listen, including radio talk shows, that they were being placed on hold for an hour or more to reach a live voice. In response, Shopping.com doubled its support staff to fifty people, at a cost exceeding $1.5 million (a major commitment, given the fact that its total revenues through the nine months ending October 1999 were just $4 million).

Another straw in the wind to observe in "shopping cart" companies (including most big names in retail) is the provision for taking an item out of the shopping cart on the way to electronic checkout. Companies used to make this process quite easy. But, according to *Forbes,* "Web sellers have noticed that online buyers are indecisive, filling up their digital shopping baskets as they proceed through a site but then erasing two-thirds of their purchases before reaching the checkout. They lose their nerve or can't find their way out." Check out your competitors' processes in this regard. Must a customer dump the whole shopping cart and start over if he or she decides to take a few items out before checkout? What practice will you employ in your business planning to encourage customers to buy most or all of the items they've placed in their carts?

Notice as well your competitors' preferred delivery systems. Do they force a customer to use a particular delivery channel unless the customer pays extra (as does Amazon.

com, with its de rigueur use of U.S. Post Office Priority Mail)? Or have your competitors come up with cost-saving approaches to product delivery, as in the case of beyond.com, which sends much of the software it sells directly by phone lines to the customer's computer rather than taking on the expense of packaging and mailing?

Also watch for compliments or testimonials paid by companies, especially when they are associated with links to other computer services. One innovative company, positions.com, has made a thriving business out of helping its clients come up first in the long string of matches that result from a Web search. This practice has been commonplace in the Yellow Pages for decades. Plumbing services, for example, will name themselves AAAAAA Plumbing just to be placed first in the alphabetical ranking within their category. Virtually all research of consumer choices shows that companies appearing at or near the beginning of a list are much more likely to be contacted by customers than those near the middle or end of the list. Positions.com is often thanked on the Web pages of its clients, and perhaps a fee reduction of some kind is involved in such a reference.

Finally, be on the lookout for that "something extra" that the most successful of your competitors offer. Kevin Jones, president of Net Market Makers, a business-to-business consulting firm, found one such striking innovation where he least expected it: in the lots of Mississippi car dealers.

As a businessperson familiar with literally hundreds of specific exchanges for products and services of all kinds, Jones was particularly impressed with the creative adaptation to a changing market accomplished by Peggy Hooks, a print publisher. Hooks had made her living for years from a small but profitable niche publication for car dealers throughout the state of Mississippi. Her reports listed the make, model, franchise, region, and other facts about new-car sales.

One large car dealer canceled his subscription, and Hooks took the time to discover why. The dealer explained that he didn't have the time to make good use of her detailed information and analyses. What the dealer really wanted, Hooks learned, was a letter-writing service: someone to contact recent car buyers with an offer to do warranty work. In addition, the dealer wanted to contact each of his new-car buyers to encourage them to contact him, not the factory, in case of problems or other needs.

Hooks had the foresight to seize this opportunity to "shift paradigms" from a product-based information business to a service-based company. She has now expanded to write promotional letters for a cellular phone company that offers new Lexus buyers a special deal on a cell phone.

Jones points out that "since Hooks's service provided a low-cost stream of incremental revenue for each dealer, she and her customers have become inextricably wed to each other.... This is the model that will work in business-to-business e-commerce: becoming the invisible plumbing behind every sale, integrated into the day-to-day processes of buying and selling."

Summing Up Step 4

EXAMINING YOUR COMPETITION IN DETAIL TAKES TIME, energy, and courage. "What I don't know can't hurt me," some entrepreneurs falsely assure themselves. It's only human to become excited about the bubble of one's e-business idea (especially when you and others have invested in it) and not want to burst it by finding out about the strengths of your competitors. But the fortitude to examine the operations of other entrants into your marketplace will pay extraordinary dividends in the later development of your e-business. You will not go blindly down business paths that others have found to be either dead ends or crowded commercial channels. It is highly recommended that you follow the numbered steps for competitor investigation contained in this chapter. If information or questions arise that take you beyond these steps, by all means pursue those leads. Your goal is to build your success on the shoulders of those who have already worked in your field.

5

STEP 5

Formalize and Conceptually Test Your Business Idea

AFTER YOU'VE THOUGHT through what you want to do vis-à-vis your competitors, as reviewed in preceding chapters, your e-business probably runs just fine in your head. In this chapter, it's time to set your ideas down on paper to see if the gears still mesh smoothly.

Relax, you're not writing a full-blown business plan—yet. Instead, the short (perhaps four to five pages), written description you will produce at first will firm up some of the fundamentals of your e-business idea. The act of writing has a wonderful way of forcing you to make decisions and eliminate ambiguity. You can call this most valuable document your "Working Plan." Don't worry if it is less than publishable; the important point is that it expresses your full vision of what you want your e-business to be.

Example of a Working Plan

IN THE FOLLOWING PLAIN-LANGUAGE STATEMENT, two recent college graduates set down the main points of their e-business idea. Instead of focusing on the specific content of their ideas, which will of course differ from yours, look instead at the *categories* these young entrepreneurs considered in shaping their Working Plan. These will probably turn out to be some of the main categories that will appear in your Working Plan as well (see pages 76–79).

Using Your Working Plan

YOU NOW HAVE BEFORE YOU A BRIEF DOCUMENT THAT accomplishes several purposes. First, it tests your ability to express your whole idea (rather than leaving it where so many good ideas expire—on a cocktail napkin). Second, you have a clear explana-

Working Plan for TeleCycle

1 Our Basic E-Business Idea

By the beginning of the new century, recycling has grown to be a profitable and socially approved industry, as Americans become more sensitized to and motivated by environmental concerns. Glass recycling, for example, has grown to a $2 billion business, with average net profits per major firm in the 11 to 12 percent range. Aluminum recycling showed a total profit of $894 million for six companies in fiscal 1999.

The TeleCycle concept involves a similar appeal, using Internet and e-mail channels, to Americans to recycle the old telephones they are no longer using. These dial phones, tone and pulse phones, and (increasingly) cellular phones—an estimated total of 38 million units—are omnipresent in the closets and on the storage shelves of American homes and businesses. The vast majority of these telephones will find their way eventually to the trash.

These phones are being replaced in record numbers by new telephones purchased by the American public. National Data Corporation estimates that 65 million new phones (of all types) were sold in America in 2000. We believe that Americans buying new phones will be more than glad to dispose of their old phones for a $5 rebate. Americans not buying new phones at this time can receive the same $5 rebate toward the purchase of a new phone within 24 months.

TeleCycle will supervise the collection of these old phones at new telephone offices and stores throughout the country. TeleCycle will assume responsibility and expense for ground shipment of these phones to a central collection warehouse in Oakland, California. There they will be divided by type (dial, cellular, etc.) and sold in bulk to interested companies in developing countries, particularly those in Central America, South America, Africa, China, and portions of the former U.S.S.R.

We anticipate that the $5 rebate will be paid by the telephone office or store collecting the old phones. This is an inexpensive way to attract customers to purchase a new telephone. Profit to TeleCycle will result from gross revenues for the international sale of telephones minus the cost of transportation and overhead.

2 A Description of Our Products and Services

Although TeleCycle will collect and pack old telephones for shipment, the company will make no representation regarding their condition, nor will the company undertake repairs of any kind. Customers will be advised that they are buying old telephones in "as-is" condition.

Based on test market studies, we estimate that 80 percent of these trade-in telephones will be in working order. Of the remaining 20 percent, we estimate that half will be easily repairable (less than $2 in parts and ten minutes of technician time), and the other half will be useful only as parts.

All evaluation, sorting, and packing of telephones will take place at TeleCycle's proposed dockside warehouse in Oakland, California.

3 How We Plan to Conduct Our E-Business

According to 1999 United Nations reports, at least forty-five creditworthy countries maintain open orders for as many telephones as they can buy in the $6 to $8 range for their internal telephone systems. Depending on availability, the commodities market of sorts for used telephones has seen prices range from $4.50 to $10 per unit in 1,000-unit lots for the period 1996 to 1999. For the period 2000 to 2003, we project an average wholesale cost per unit for used telephones to be $8 and have based financial assumptions on that projection.

(continued on the following page)

Working Plan for TeleCycle (cont.)

TeleCycle will contact major buyers of used telephone equipment, both private and public, in selected countries from the United Nations list of frequent telephone buyers. Preliminary contacts with ten foreign commercial officers attached to their embassies in Washington, D.C., have provided us with several bona fide purchase offers for used telephones in large lots. We also have had strong international interest in the purchase of telephone parts and recyclable electronic materials.

We will create and maintain an attractive, functional Web site that tells the TeleCycle story and provides click-through contact options for (1) those interested in buying telephones, (2) distribution sites willing to collect old telephones, and (3) others who wish to contact the principals at TeleCycle. The Web site will display the number of telephones collected so far. We are contemplating a series of prizes for the cities that collect the most phones.

4 How We Plan to Market Our Products

TeleCycle will market its services in four distinct ways:

- Decision makers at the majority of new telephone sales-and-distribution centers will be contacted by telephone and, simultaneously, will be given a prospectus and proposal for partnership in the collection of old telephones.
- Follow-up visits and calls will be made by TeleCycle principals to bring these distributors (Pacific Bell, GTE, Bellsouth, AT&T, etc.) aboard as contracted partners.
- Advertising on Internet sites, and in foreign trade journals, magazines, and newspapers will alert foreign buyers of telephones to this opportunity. Written expression of their interest will be used to further convince American telephone distributors to join the program.
- Once a threshold number of American distributors have contracted with TeleCycle, we will begin a nationwide

publicity campaign telling people how and where to recycle their old telephones for the $5 rebate. Our initial contacts with the Environmental Protection Agency and the Advertising Council give us strong reason to believe that many of these advertisements may be carried by the media as low-cost or no-cost public interest ads.

When a stable network of collection sites has been arranged, TeleCycle will enter into contracts for the sale of used telephones with qualified foreign buyers.

5 How We Will Make Money

Based on a per-unit profit of 60 percent after handling, shipping, and overhead, TeleCycle projects the following volume and revenues for years 1, 2, and 3:

YEAR	UNITS SOLD	GROSS INCOME	NET PROFIT
1	90,000	$ 720,000	$ 432,000
2	200,000	1,600,000	930,000
3	340,000	2,720,000	1,632,000

6 Management of the Company

TeleCycle will be directed by two MBAs with substantial experience both in the telephone industry and in international sales. *[Biographical information of the principals appears here.]*

7 How We Will Attract Seed Capital

For investors interested in one or more units (at $25,000 per unit) of this venture, we will provide copies of a contractual limited partnership. Individual investors each may own up to four units. The company seeks to place a total of twenty units with investors.

tion you can share with partners to make sure you are all "on the same page" regarding your development ideas. Third, you have a mini–business plan you can test, in ways described in the remainder of this chapter. Finally, your Working Plan takes you more than halfway toward the completion of your complete business plan (an outline of this important document appears at the end of the chapter).

It's crucial to put the ideas in your Working Plan to one or more tests before you invest your or others' money in actualizing the plan. Here are two proven testing techniques that will cost you little or no money but can yield dramatic improvements in your plans for your e-business.

KING ARTHUR'S ROUNDTABLE

YOU HAVE A FEW BUSINESS-SAVVY FRIENDS WHO CAN BE trusted not to steal or tell others about your e-business idea. Ask these people to give you two hours of their time (a nice meal afterwards is a good trade-off) and some of their best critical thinking. Seat them around a table and present each of them with a copy of your Working Plan. Ask them to take twenty minutes or so to read the plan and briefly discuss it with one another. Tell them you will return to the room to answer any preliminary questions after twenty minutes. Do not provide any other explanations, coaching, justifications, or other buffering before you leave the room while they read and discuss the plan.

When you return to the room, take notes on each of their questions. Provide brief, nondefensive answers. (Don't say, for example, "You just don't understand" or "In real business it doesn't happen that way.") Your goal is to encourage inquiry into your Working Plan by fresh eyes. After this brief question-and-answer session (no more than five minutes), ask the participants to discuss the plan as if they were being asked to become investors (they aren't—it's just a useful role for analysis).

The primary task for members of the group is to discuss the likely success and practical feasibility of your e-business idea. What do they like? What don't they like? Where do they think you're right or wrong? Tell them their conversation will be tape-recorded so that you can benefit from their thoughts, pro and con. Let them know this is a no-holds-barred discussion—you would rather have frank, honest criticism than a lot of misspent money and effort later. If the group is sensitive about being tape-recorded, tell them you will destroy the tape after listening to it and perhaps transcribing it.

Later, as you listen to the tape, take careful notes. Avoid the inclination to hear what you want to hear. Instead, think through each of the difficult issues that participants raise. If possible, check back with a few of the participants to make sure you understood their points completely.

In my experience, every e-business founder who has conscientiously carried through the King Arthur's Roundtable test goes on to make significant improvements in the Working Plan and eventual Business Plan. If you are in a corporate setting, of course, you can easily alter this testing approach and the following one by selecting a blue-ribbon committee as your participants. Be sure to draw them from various divisions or departments in your company and to designate at least one to play the role of customer.

SHARPSHOOTING

WE ALL KNOW AT LEAST ONE PERSON WE CONSIDER, WELL, damn smart. The person may not have technical expertise in your field, but they seem to "think well" no matter what the topic of conversation. If you have such a person in your circle of friends or business acquaintances, ask him or her for an hour or two to play sharpshooter with your Working Plan. (In the case of acquaintances, you may have to offer some money for this service, much as in a consulting arrangement. The money is well spent.) Specifically, you will ask this bright person to read your Working Plan, then to pretend that he or she is hell-bent on competing successfully against your e-business and perhaps eventually putting you out of business. Ask the person to sketch out one or more competition strategies that have the potential to injure your business efforts or even blow you out of the water.

Once these strategies are developed, sit down with the

person and talk them through. It should be your role to tell how you would counter the strategy—and the bright person (you are, too, of course) will play along to show how he or she would counterattack. This good-natured debate will give you a valuable glimpse of actual strategies that may be launched against your e-business, especially if it rises quickly to profitability or "gores someone else's ox" on its way to success.

Once your e-business is up and running on the Web, there are other tests and measurements that can give you important information about the wisdom of your business approach and planning. Such measures are discussed in Step 12. For now, use the information you glean from King Arthur's Roundtable and sharpshooting to undertake a top-to-bottom revision of your Working Plan.

From Working Plan to Business Plan

THE WORKING PLAN IS AN INTERNAL DOCUMENT USED PRIMARILY for discussion and orientation of new partners and employees. The Business Plan is an external document, written to the precise specifications of the audience you hope to persuade. Let's say, for example, that you plan to approach a venture capital (VC) group for seed money to begin your e-business. In most cases, the VC group will have a particular length in mind for business plans they are willing to read. This length varies widely—one San Francisco VC company insists that a business plan be no more than five pages. The principals then give the would-be entrepreneur no more than ten minutes to present the contents of those five pages. Other VC companies allow more latitude in length and design. The important point, however, is to check with your intended audience for recommended document models and required content categories before writing your business plan.

You may also be writing your business plan for less-sophisticated investors, including relatives and friends who may turn out to be financial partners. In that case, keep business jargon to a minimum. Make all financial explanations crystal clear (perhaps stating them both in words and as graphs or charts). You don't want any of your investors to misunderstand what you are committing to or what they are required to do.

OUTSOURCING THE WRITING, IF NECESSARY

IF YOU AREN'T A RELATIVE OF SHAKESPEARE AND NEED writing assistance, a local business professor involved in business planning may be willing to consult for a reasonable fee as lead writer on your business plan. If you do involve help of this kind, keep your own finger in the pie during all stages. No one knows your business idea as well as you do. Good writing is meaningless without your good thinking to support it.

Across industries, the categories described in the following section almost always appear in business plans. After investigating the document needs of the audience to whom you are addressing the business plan, set your sights on a relatively short document (ten to twenty pages). You can always beef up sections in the plan to make it longer if required.

COMPONENTS OF AN E-BUSINESS PLAN

IN ORDER, HERE ARE THE COMMONLY RECOMMENDED COMponents of a professional business plan:

- **Title Page.** With entries usually centered and spaced attractively for a balanced page, the title page includes (in order, top to bottom) the name of the business ("E-Circuits.com"), the phrase "Business Plan," the phrase "submitted to" followed by the company name or individual names of the audience, and the word "by" and the name(s) of the individuals or organization submitting the plan. Near the bottom of the title page is the date of submission, and beneath the date an appropriate warning phrase about the use of the document, for example, "Proprietary Information." In some cases, your legal counsel may advise you to have readers sign a nondisclosure agreement regarding the contents of your plan before reviewing it.
- **Table of Contents.** This is a listing of the main categories and page numbers within your business plan. A table of

contents is usually omitted if the business plan is fewer than ten pages.

- **Executive Summary.** Face it: some busy decision makers won't read every word of your plan. This first, crucial page gives these fast-trackers the chance to understand your core concept in one page of reading, then to skim the rest of the plan for other details.

  In your executive summary, include a brief description of the product and/or service, why it is marketable using e-business strategies and technologies, possible future demands for the product or service, a summary of the financial goals of your proposal, and an overview of the current position of the company and the personnel involved in the project.
- **Description of Proposed Products and Services.** Fully describe what you have to offer the market in terms of products and/or services: where these stand in their life cycles (for example, are they new or a revised version of an existing product or service), the present status of patents or copyrights, and future plans for product research. Emphasize why the Internet is an attractive vehicle for your products or services.
- **Provisions for Manufacturing and Distribution.** Describe the manufacturing process, even if it is outsourced: how complex the operations are and what logistics are required, what the production capacity is, and who the intended suppliers are. In addition, spell out the distribution system in an e-business setting.
- **Marketing Plan.** The marketing plan is a critical segment of the business plan. Cite facts on the industry in which the product is competing and the present sales trends. Present firm data on Internet and e-business aspects of your intended marketing. What are the short-term and long-term profit potentials?

  In addition, a specific marketing plan should identify the market segment(s) targeted. Include a customer profile as well as an analysis of market needs, market segments, and sales by geographical areas or Internet audience divisions, and explain how these segments will change with time, increased competition, and environmental, social, and economic changes. Also include in the marketing section a brief analysis of how and why this marketing plan is not only different from but also superior to that of competitors.

- **E-Business Operations.** Describe the day-to-day operation of the e-business you propose. What must be managed or inspected or monitored? Who will do what in helping move the business toward success and growth? Where will such operations take place? What physical growth in terms of office space is anticipated? What technological growth can be foreseen to keep the company current?
- **Financial Information.** Include a financial statement, if available, for the year to date. Develop projections for the next three years and, if possible, beyond. These projections should cover sales, cost of sales, cash flow, pro forma balance sheets, and key statistics (current ratio, debt-equity ratio, and inventory turnovers). Include in this section any legal disclosure you must make about pending lawsuits by or against the organization, the potential for liability, insurance coverage in force or needed, and related areas.
- **Management Personnel.** List the key members of management with a summary of their personal backgrounds, work experiences (especially in e-business), education, and any other areas relevant to their jobs. The reader should conclude from this section of the business plan that the company has sufficient human talent to achieve the goals it has set for itself. In a time of tight labor markets, many business plans also include a short section explaining how new employees will be recruited and hired.
- **Business Offering.** Bound within the business plan or attached as a separate document, include a succinct statement of the financial arrangements you are offering to investors or venture capitalists in your proposed e-business. What do they commit to give or do? What do you promise in return? Although such terms usually go through a process of negotiation, you have the chance to take the first stab at setting the investment agenda by setting forth your preferred terms in the business plan.

In their first substantial appearance in the 1990s, e-business plans looked somewhat different from traditional business plans. The former tended to be definitive about technical details (Web site architecture, programming platforms, and so forth) and vague about marketing plans, analysis of the competition, and description of day-to-day operations. The prevailing attitude was "Build it, and they will come."

Since the arrival of the new century, however, venture capitalists and other investors have demanded that e-business plans return to the thoroughgoing descriptions and metrics expected of Old Economy businesses. Since the vast majority of e-businesses have failed within their first year, potential investors and readers of e-business plans are not willing to allow enthusiasm in the business plan to take the place of careful analysis. Therefore, at present the e-business plan follows very much the same pattern of argument and presentation as the traditional business plan, with the addition, of course, of sufficient technical detail to convey the author's competence in Web site creation and management.

If writing a business plan sounds like hard work, you're listening well. For that reason, many of the most promising e-business plans are left to die in verbal form ("Let me tell you about a great idea...") or are sketched out only on a cocktail napkin. The difficulty of composing a business plan includes not only the task of writing, which few of us enjoy, but also the job of thinking well. An e-business that can't be cogently described in a business plan probably will be even more disorganized if it is rushed to the Web.

Summing Up Step 5

LIKE A HIGH-RESOLUTION PHOTOGRAPH, A GOOD BUSINESS plan gives you a chance to see not only the attractive features of your e-business concept but also its wrinkles and flaws. The working business plan is not a public relations or sales document written to convince others to invest in or hire on to your business. Instead, this document is a thorough map that answers the basic questions of any business venture: What do you seek to do? How will you do it? What barriers do you face, and how will they be overcome? What risks exist, and how can they be minimized? What profits are likely? Who will run the business? Until you think through and write down careful answers to such questions, you cannot be sure that your e-business concept is more than a pipe dream.

6

STEP 6

Protect Your E-Business Concept

A GREAT DEAL HAS BEEN WRITten about "scanning" techniques by which people listen in on others' cellular telephone conversations, hacking strategies by which private e-mail is read by others, and code-breaking algorithms that allow unauthorized access to encrypted data.

Wait a minute! The big leak for valuable information is one human being blabbing to another. Now that you have or are preparing to expose your e-business idea to many others in the form of a Working Plan and Business Plan, what can you do to protect your intellectual property from idea thieves?

The Flap over E-Business Patents

THE FIRST THING YOU WILL HEAR WHEN YOU RAISE the topic of e-business patents or copyrights in social conversation is something along these lines: "How can you think of patenting an e-business technique or strategy? The Internet belongs to everyone!" A similar answer was given in the late 1800s when inventors tried to patent agricultural inventions—"The fields belong to God!"—and in the 1960s when pharmaceutical companies sought to patent certain drugs—"They belong to all of us!"

E-business, too, faces a baptism of fire as its entrepreneurs attempt to protect aspects of their operations and technologies from intrusion by others. Richard Poynder, author of *Hidden Value—How Intellectual Property Know-how Can Make or Break Your Business* (Derwent Information, 1999), tells the story of one such e-company: "Massachusetts-based Open Market has been granted several patents that, some claim, could potentially allow it to demand royalties from almost any company engaged in e-commerce. These include a patent on a secure, real-time payment method using debit and credit cards, one covering electronic shopping carts, and another on a technique for analyzing how users browse Web content. To date, Open Market has not taken legal action against supposed infringers.

"In contrast, Sightsound.com—which claims to have been granted a patent that covers the sale of any digital audio or video recording over the Internet—is currently suing N2K, a company that retails music on the Web. The Mt. Lebanon, Pennsylvania, company has also written to a number of other prominent music sites demanding royalties on every sale that involves downloading music to a customer. CEO Scott Sander insists that Sightsound.com is only seeking the same reward any inventor would expect: 'Sony and Philips received a royalty for each compact disc that was sold while their patents on CD technology were in force,' he says. 'We're seeking the same right.'"

Underlying all this infighting is a 1998 Federal Circuit Court of Appeals ruling that allows patents for business methods. One of the most prominent companies to take advantage of this ruling is Priceline.com. It claims to have patent rights on "reverse auctions" in which buyers set a price for a product or service and sellers bid to supply it. The quality of novelty seems to be a key determinant in whether the U.S. Patent Office will act favorably on such applications. One business method judged sufficiently novel for its own patent was Cybergold's idea of pay-per-view advertising (in which users are paid for looking at Internet-based advertising).

If most of the basic technologies now used on the Internet are awarded to particular companies, the viability of e-business itself may be threatened. Cary Sherman, senior vice president of the Recording Industry Association of America, puts the situation well: "You may have to use compression technologies, watermarking technologies, encryption technologies, clearinghouse technologies—all of which could be an essential component of a digital distribution system. Paying royalties on all these technologies adds up, and represents a significant cost factor."

Evaluating Your Need for Patents and Copyrights

FIRST, LET'S GET OUR TERMS STRAIGHT ABOUT INTELLECTUAL property, copyright, trade secrets, and patents.

Intellectual property refers to ideas, plans, concepts, and other intangible property created by individuals or corporations and protected under laws related to copyright, trade secrets, and patents.

Copyright gives the creator of the work ownership of it for twenty-eight years and the right to collect fees from anyone who makes copies or otherwise uses the work. Every word and image on your Web site can be legitimately copyrighted simply by affixing a copyright notice to your site. The usual form for such a copyright statement, typically placed at the bottom of the Web page, is "Copyright ©[Year] [Your Name]. All rights reserved." The familiar © symbol is usually included but is not technically required for a legal copyright.

In addition to the content of a Web page, some forms of source and object codes have been granted copyright protection by the U.S. Federal Computer Software Copyright Act of 1980. But left in legal limbo is the ownership status of such common computer functions as pull-down menus, click-through ordering, use of icons, and patterns of color.

A trade secret is a form of intellectual property (such as a recipe, business plan, or market strategy) developed by a company from its own resources, not from publicly available information. Your e-business plan is probably eligible for protection as your trade secret.

A patent gives the holder the right to determine the use and financial royalties stemming from an invention for a period of seventeen years. The U.S. Patent Office now lists thousands of patents related to Internet technologies. Juno Online Services, for example, was able to patent its interactive ad approach. Open Market successfully patented its digital active advertising and network sales systems.

If you believe your e-business plan incorporates novel, innovative technologies or strategies that deserve protection as your intellectual property, see an intellectual property attorney familiar with Internet issues and litigation. At the same time, if you feel you are in danger of using technologies or strategies already patented or copyrighted by someone else, have an intellectual property attorney do a thorough review of your proposed e-business system before rolling it out on the Internet. The dollars you will spend for wise legal counsel are few in comparison to potential fines and settlements that could arise from being sued.

Short of copyrighting or patenting your programming, downloadable files, graphics, and other components of your e-business, you can brand each with a digital watermark. (Use this search word to discover many businesses on the Web that provide watermarking services. Among such services are www.adobe.com and www.signafy.com.) A watermark is an invisible bit of digital code embedded in your source code and other programming. The watermark becomes inseparable from such data. If others pirate your materials for their own use, you will be able to prove your original ownership of those materials by uncovering the hidden watermark. Many pirates of copyrighted music have been caught and sued by the discovery of the original artist's watermark in the stolen music.

The newest legislation affecting all e-businesses is the Digital Millennium Copyright Act of 1998. As summarized by professor Efraim Turban and his colleagues, the legislation:

- reasserts copyright in cyberspace.
- makes illegal most attempts to defeat anticopying technology.
- requires the National Telecommunications and Information Administration to review the effect the bill would have on the free flow of information and make recommendations for any changes two years after it is signed into law.
- lets companies and common citizens circumvent anticopying technology when necessary to make software or hardware compatible with other products, to conduct encryption research, or to keep personal information from being spread by Internet cookies or other copy-protected tools.
- forbids excessive copying of databases, even when those

databases contain information already in the public domain.

What does this legislation mean to the small-business e-commerce entrepreneur? In essence, the Copyright Act of 1998 gives warning to thieves of your specific Web site content, databases, and programming that they may be prosecuted in federal court, with significant criminal penalties. In the same way under earlier copyright law that you could not legally photocopy a book and republish it as your own, now it is clear that others cannot rip off core aspects of your Web site and thereby clone your business without your permission.

A Controversial Case Involving Intellectual Property

WHEN YOU REGISTERED YOUR DOMAIN NAME (PROBABLY ENDing in .com or .net or .org), you probably did so through a company called Network Solutions, Inc. (NSI). Until June 1, 1998, NSI operated under an exclusive contract from the U.S. government to assign domain addresses, the most common of which are .com, .net, .mil, .gov, .edu, and .org. Under pressure from the European Council of Registrars (CORE), NSI gave up its exclusive right to issue domain names on June 1, 1998, and now shares a common registration system with several competing companies.

CORE, working with the Global Internet Project, wants to revise the domain designation system to repair what it perceives as current problems in the World Wide Web. For example, it would like to restrict all purveyors of pornography on the Web to a distinguishing "dot" designator (.sex, perhaps). Labeled in this way, such sites could easily be locked out of some systems, let's say, to protect children. It is the current state of affairs on the Web that entirely unpredictable search words—"mummify," for example—may turn up a bevy of hard-core sex sites in addition to the information a child or other person might be seeking.

Another controversy that continues to plague NSI and its companion companies has to do with the domain names that have been granted to many companies. Let's say you are the chairman of the board of McDonald's Corporation. Over the years you have spent millions of dollars to make Ronald McDonald a recognizable name and face to virtually every American. A start-up toy company, let's say, seeks a catchy, useful domain name for its launch on the Internet. It applies for and receives the domain name ronaldmcdonald.com. Fair? Certainly not, you probably say. That name rightly belongs to the McDonald's Corporation. And who should be sued if the name is given to someone else? The toy company requesting the name? The domain-granting company approving and assigning the name?

This issue is not at all hypothetical. DC Comics for years has featured a comic hero named Brainiac among its comic book characters. Another company, Brainiac Services Inc., with no relation or royalty to DC Comics, uses the comic character's name in its Internet domain. The eventual court settlement of this case will be an important precedent in the ongoing struggle to define and enforce intellectual property protections on the Internet.

Obtaining a Trademark

YOUR COMPANY NAME (INCLUDING YOUR URL, OR DOT-COM address) can be trademarked (that is, reserved for your sole use) under federal law for fifteen years, and it is renewable thereafter. Unique names of your products and services can similarly be trademarked. You would feel cheated, no doubt, if your investment of time and money in publicizing your "Wee Folks" dolls was stolen by a competitor who took the name and concept as his or her own. Protect yourself from these all-too-common occurrences by registering all trademarkable names, phrases, labels, and logos with the U.S. Patent and Trademark Office, accessible online at www.uspto.gov/teas/e-TEAS/index.html.

You will find that individual states also have trademark registration processes, allowing, for example, a drapery cleaner in Texas to have the name Best Drape Cleaning without running afoul of the same name used in Maine by another, unrelated drape cleaning company. But the Internet spans not only states but countries. You will want to protect your valuable names, labels, logos, and other items in as broad a jurisdiction as possible.

Protecting Your Business and Your Customers: E-Business Security

PROBABLY THE MOST INFAMOUS COMPUTER HACKER OF THEM all, Kevin Mitnick, was arrested in 1995 after penetrating computers and telephone switches of the country's largest companies and most sensitive government organizations. Proclaimed Mitnick, "Computers can be broken into. If they are on the Internet, they might as well have a welcome mat."

In the remainder of this chapter you will read about the dark side of communication freedom on the Internet. As you consider each of the electronic risks described here, apply them to the e-business you are about to launch.

In spite of remarkable technological achievements in encryption and "fire walls" (discussed later), both e-business owners and customers continue to run very real risks when conducting business on the Internet. Consider six areas of vulnerability:

1 **Theft and fraud.** An intruder gains access to your financial records and passwords, then transfers funds to another account, probably outside this country. To hide his tracks, the intruder makes a digital mess of your records. Expensive computer consultants must be brought in to help you get your business and finances back together.

2 **Information theft.** You store in your e-business computer files extensive information on clients, credit, trade secrets, products, company finances, and your marketplace. In the wrong hands, this information can embarrass you at the least and devastate your business and reputation at the worst. Once connected illegally to your system, a hacker may need no more than a few seconds to download highly proprietary information. That information can be sold to others or, just as bad, broadcast indiscriminately on the Web (as embarrassing memos, pictures, and other materials often have been in the past year).

3 **Business interruption.** Over a period of one week in mid-February 2000, computing systems at Amazon.com, eBay, E*Trade, and Yahoo!, among others, fell prey to a sustained hacking attack that brought usual business on these popular sites to a virtual standstill. Just as the attack began on Yahoo!, AT&T security expert Steve Bellovin was giving a speech at the offices of a large Internet service provider. One of his Powerpoint slides read, "What are the strong defenses?" The next slide said, "There aren't any."

In this particular incident, so-called black-hat hackers (who spread cyber-chaos just for their fun) electronically commandeered many powerful computers around the country and instructed them to barrage the target computers of Yahoo! and others with requests and messages. Explains Joe Minarik, an executive at Excite, "It's as if you've got a phone line that can handle 100 calls, and they drive 1,000 to it."

Business losses? You bet. Amazon.com alone lost millions of dollars' worth of business during the interruption, and total losses to the targeted companies may have exceeded $1 billion. But that amount was spare change compared to the economic impact of a much larger hack-attack, the "I Love You" message that jammed thousands of computers in May 2000. The damage in lost business and compromised information in that debacle exceeded $10 billion. Because you're not establishing an Amazon.com does not mean that you are immune from such attacks. This chapter concludes with a discussion of fire walls, insurance, and other means by which you can plan for and minimize the business damage that such cyber-nuts can do.

Business interruption can also come, of course, through failure of your server (a not uncommon event, as you may know from experience in any major business or university), glitches in programming for your own business, or severe weather events, such as floods, tornadoes, hurricanes, and so forth, that destroy server hubs.

4 **Stolen resources.** You get a phone bill that exponentially exceeds your usual bill. You discover that your computing system has been laboring away on a huge task (perhaps the mass mailing of an obscene message to half the world) that

you certainly did not authorize. That is an example of resource theft. An unauthorized user of your business system can quite easily turn your considerable computing power to his or her own purposes.

5 **Lost reputation and customer relationships.** How many computer failures does it take to make you look for another supplier? Banks have discovered that customers often begin to look for another financial institution if they are told more than twice that their requests or transactions cannot be honored "because our computers are down." Patience for this sort of failure is wearing thin among the public. You don't want it to be said about your e-business in customer chat rooms or e-mails that "their prices are good, but you can never get through. They have a lousy customer interface."

6 **Cleanup expenses.** Finally, a very real consideration related to breakdowns in your electronic security is the expense, in terms of money, time, and energy, of tracking down and correcting corrupted orders, shipments, billing, tax records, and other files.

THE ABCs OF SECURITY FOR YOUR E-BUSINESS

YOU INVITE CUSTOMERS TO SHOP AT YOUR E-BUSINESS. CAN they be confident that unauthorized outsiders are not peeking over their shoulders as they fill their baskets, reveal their credit card numbers, and key in their PINs or passwords?

The answer, with qualification, is yes. Here's how your browser keeps such information private. Before sending entered data back to your server and Web site, the browser encrypts it—in effect, scrambles or codes it in such a way that it cannot be understood by a cyber-eavesdropper. The most common method for encrypting data is the Secure Sockets Layer, or SSL, method. If you use Netscape or Internet Explorer, look for the closed-lock symbol on the status bar to know whether your message is being sent using SSL encryption. Or look at the URL in the Location box. It begins with https:// instead of the standard http://. The additional *s* stands for the word "Secure" in "HyperText Transport Protocol Secure."

In simplified form, encryption works like this. A series of digits is attached at the end of the original text. This series of digits means nothing until it is unlocked by a mathematical key at the reception end. Let's say I attached the digit 9 to the end of the message "Hello." My message is sent in scrambled form as "Khoor." The key at the reception end happens to be a 3. When the key 3 is applied to the encryption digit 9, a quick arithmetic operation is performed: 9 divided by 3 equals 3. That result means that each letter in the scrambled message "Khoor" needs to be "backed up" by three places to find the correct, or unencrypted, message. Thus "Khoor" again becomes "Hello." (This approach uses the so-called Caesar Cypher method. There are many others.)

Now put yourself in the place of a hacker with nothing better to do than pry into other people's messages and steal their access codes to their financial resources. What would you do if you were able to surreptitiously observe the scrambled message "Khoor-9"? Obviously, you would begin dividing the number 9 and seeing if the application of the resulting answer would make sense out of the message.

Can encryption protect us against this kind of "see-what-works" experimentation by hackers? The answer lies in simply making the attached number longer. A 40-bit key number is now used in the international version of Netscape Communicator, and the U.S. version uses a 128-bit key. Could the most powerful computer, working around the clock, find the right mathematical relationship to unlock this encryption? Well, yes—but it's estimated that processing time for such calculations would be several centuries. That's secure enough for me.

It makes sad sense, in this regard, that China has strict laws against the use of certain types of encryption for messages and data passing in and out of the country as well as within the country. The powers-that-be want to be able to break into any message anytime for reasons of "security," broadly interpreted. Our own export laws have regulations about exporting some of the more sophisticated encryption systems.

LET ME SEE YOUR DIGITAL CERTIFICATE

A NEW WRINKLE IN SECURED TRANSACTIONS IS THE DIGITAL certificate. This is an ID that verifies the identity of the user or owner of a Web site. To open a secure connection with your site, you must supply your browser with a copy of your digital certificate. Labels aside, digital certificates are not pieces of paper like diplomas. Instead, they are pass codes provided by companies such as VeriSign; these companies are responsible for verifying that the digital certificate being used does in fact belong to the authorized party. Johnson & Johnson, which must communicate much sensitive medical information over the Internet and other channels, uses a version of the digital certificate in which the appropriate password changes every few seconds. A message sender transmits a message using the password that is "up" for that moment. The password will be meaningless and useless a few seconds later.

The most common and "breakable" form of security for your customer is the familiar authentication routine used on most sign-up screens, including those of eBay, Amazon.com, and Yahoo!. The user is asked to enter a user name (often the person's e-mail user name) and a self-chosen password. If these match, the Web server will be given the OK to move on to the next Web page.

Although this authentication system will probably remain the most common point of entry for some time to come, it is vulnerable in several ways. First, your e-mail address (as a user name) is easy to obtain from company directories, business cards, college listings, and many other sources. Once a person has that user name, he or she can begin guessing your password. Those guesses are not at all random. Infothieves find that people tend to use the names of partners, parts of telephone numbers or Social Security numbers, names of children, names of pets, birthdays, anniversaries, street names or addresses, or words associated with their occupations. (See if this list happens to strike home with any of your passwords!)

Can you imagine the financial damage that can be done once a thief has your user name and matching password?

It's very much like having the PIN to your automated teller account at your bank. The money just comes flowing out of your account. At e-brokerages, all that is commonly required to conduct transactions (including withdrawing potentially huge amounts of cash) is the person's user name and password. Many companies offer to e-mail people reminders of their passwords if they have forgotten them. Shrewd thieves use this to their advantage. They simply pretend to be you, then tell a company that they have forgotten "their" password. It arrives ready for use by e-mail a few seconds later.

SERVING COOKIES AND ERECTING FIRE WALLS

SOME COMPANIES, SUCH AS PHOTOPOINT.COM, USE "COOKIES" to aid in a so-called Quick Sign-on procedure. In cyberspeak, a cookie is a small text file stored on your hard drive and your browser, that acts on directions from the Web server. If you opt for Quick Sign-on at Photopoint.com, you in effect give your browser permission to plant identifying information about you (and, for other companies, your purchases, address, and the like) onto your hard drive. When you begin to sign in to these online companies, they look for the presence and contents of your cookie as a way of identifying you and setting up service for you.

Your customers have a legal right to expect that their personal information (name, address, phone, family information, credit history, income, and so on) is protected from unauthorized intrusion. E-businesses typically accomplish such protection through the use of a fire wall. This safeguard is usually a combination of hardware and software that provides an impenetrable barrier between the information stored on the Web site's computer and the outside world. The same fire wall that prevents outsiders from rooting around in your private information can also be used to prevent insiders in the company from going where they have no need to go in company files. In this use, a company employee must have a special clearance code to be able to access certain areas of stored information. The fire wall can also prevent company employees from accessing any URL they choose outside the company. Companies have been able to keep their employees from wasting time with games, risqué sites, or other nonbusiness pursuits by creating fire walls that allow access only to preselected URLs.

The small-business e-commerce entrepreneur has no less need for such fire walls than the largest companies. Many software products are available (see Appendix A) that minimize the risk of hackers and curious employees exploring your confidential personnel records, financial data, customer names and addresses, product information, salary structure, and other private data. Just as a fire wall in an automobile safely separates the engine from the passenger compartment, so a software fire wall keeps you secure from the significant damage that hacking and leaks can do. In this view, a reliable fire wall is a necessity, not a luxury, even for the smallest e-business.

SECURITY AND MONEY

BOTTOM LINE, THE ISSUE OF SECURITY ON THE WEB FOR MOST people has less to do with stolen information than with stolen money. American citizens who have grown used to giving their credit card information over the telephone (and cellular telephone) without the bat of an eye have somehow become card-shy when it comes to providing the same financial information over the Internet. This is all the more ironic given the fact that telephone messages are hardly ever encrypted (and can easily be "scanned" in the case of cellular phones), while virtually all Internet financial data is thoroughly encrypted.

Owners of e-business sites generally set up the ability to accept Visa, MasterCard, Discover, American Express, and other credit cards through their Internet service provider or through standard packages such as IBM's Startup. These prepackaged services link the site directly to credit card verifying and approval sites so that the business can determine a customer's creditworthiness almost immediately online and complete the transaction. The customer is billed by the credit card company for the amount of the purchase (without sales tax, in most cases, for Internet transactions between states), and the e-business as the merchant is credited with that amount, minus a fee (typically 4 percent or so), to its bank account.

The customer's financial data is held secure using the encryption techniques already discussed. In the near future, those transactions will be all the more secure, given the groundbreaking work done recently by Visa and MasterCard to establish the Secure Electronic Transaction standard, a protocol for data transmission that breaks the customer's financial data into separate packages that are then reassembled after transmission from the Internet.

Digital cash sites such as PayPal and CyberCash allow the user to deposit funds with the service, then authorize payment to merchants and others who are signed up with that service. The consumer bears no expense for these services, and even the merchant's traditional fee is getting smaller, as digital cash companies learn to leverage the amounts of money they hold via investments.

One of the perennial payment problems for e-businesses is how to bill for micropayments. Let's say that you have a site offering maps for any major city in the United States. You do not want to give this information away for free (banner advertising has proven less than profitable, let's assume), and so you decide to charge users the insignificant sum of 25¢ each time they get an on-screen map from your site (which they probably print out). But how do you bill users? Do they run an account until it reaches a balance of several dollars, at which time it makes sense to bill via the usual credit cards? If so, what about the customer—perhaps your typical customer—who uses your service only once a month or so? Do you wait an entire year to bill him or her a measly $3?

CyberCash and other payment services now offer a solution to this dilemma. CyberCash's innovative Cyber-Coin accepts payments in the 25¢-to-$10 range without using typical per-transaction charges.

Finally, so-called Smart Cards are being used more and more to assure secure financial transactions. Each card has a built-in microprocessor and memory chip that identifies the user and provides a transaction record. Customers no longer must remember passwords but can now simply swipe their

Smart Cards through a reader attached to their computers, much as customers now use credit and ATM cards at supermarkets and department stores. More details about the growing use of these cards can be found at ecash.com.

Internet Scams

IN MARCH 2000, *U.S. NEWS AND WORLD REPORT* ADMIRABLY summed up the seedy, seductive world of Internet scams. The subject is very much on the public's mind (and therefore should be on your radar screen as an e-business owner) because these scams are occurring increasingly in both business-to-consumer and business-to-business transactions. You might become a victim even in your dealings with those offering to help you protect or enhance your Web site.

Among the scams described by *U.S. News and World Report* was an "auto buyer" who solicited cash from customers under the pretense that the buyer would attend car auctions on their behalf and purchase a specified model of car at a low price. Customers who sent in their money waited months for such purchases, only to receive eventual notice that the buyer was having financial difficulty and could not hold up his end of the bargain or return their money. Scams such as this one work because scam artists can contact millions of possible customers through the Internet. Out of those vast numbers, it's likely that at least a few will fall for the ruse. The Internet Fraud Watch, a service of the National Consumers League, keeps track of online scams and fraud. By its calculation, such deception has increased threefold within the last year.

One of the reasons that people fall for scams on the Internet, according to Patricia Kelly, consumer protection chief for the Illinois attorney general's office, is that "no one sees you, no one talks to you, you don't know how old somebody is. You don't have any of the cues that you would have in a person-to-person contact." Nineteen people, for example, responded to a phony "Loyola State University" ad promising bachelor's, master's, and doctoral degrees for varying prices up to $2,795. Only a summary of their life experiences was required to receive a diploma.

Other common ploys include e-mail requests for credit card numbers from a supposed official source; a "free" offer that turns out to involve extraordinary telephone hookup charges and hidden fees; and "work at home" schemes that sell software or other tools but never deliver the work they describe.

The Internet also hosts a myriad of home cures and elixirs, some of them quite dangerous. *The New England Journal of Medicine* recently reported the case of a patient who had purchased poisonous wormwood oil over the Internet after seeing it advertised there for kidney problems. He consumed the oil and almost died of acute kidney failure. Although the vast majority of scam artists on the Internet are never caught, the Federal Trade Commission is acting aggressively to track and prosecute Internet criminals. The commission holds regular "surf days" devoted to scanning the Internet for scams. In March 2000, the FTC sent warnings to 200 e-businesses that appeared to be guilty of making exaggerated or deceptive claims. Within a month, almost 50 of those firms had mended their ways.

Self-policing is also showing promise in reducing the number of Internet-based scam operations. Interactive Services Association is promoting a seal of approval for members, who must promise to abide by a code of conduct. Some Internet service providers impose fines on members who clog e-mail channels with chain letters and junk mail. After the August 2000 precipitous drop of almost 100 points in the price of Emulex stock due to a false rumor on the Internet, the Securities and Exchange Commission is stepping up its efforts to curtail criminal manipulation of the financial markets.

For both small-business entrepreneurs and large-company Web administrators, the first hint of a potential scam is the "cash in advance" demand by the perpetrator. This ploy may take the form of the "uncharged credit card" strategy: the crook assures the customer that his or her credit card will remain uncharged until the product or service is received and found satisfactory. In practice, however, the charge card is often billed immediately for fees far surpassing those advertised. It then becomes the customer's problem to track down and try to receive repayment from the scam artist.

Insuring Yourself against Disaster and Fraud

YOUR HOME IS INSURED AGAINST FIRE, YOUR CAR IS INSURED against damage, and your life is insured against, well, the Big Chill. Can you insure your fledgling e-business against the many vulnerabilities described in this chapter? A small but growing number of e-business insurance companies, including InsureTrust.com, offer Internet-specific insurance policies. They include coverage of malicious Internet interruptions caused by hackers and vandals. Rick Davis, co-founder of the company, says his firm's policies provide for one of the most common tactics used by computer hackers to overload a network, the "ICMP ping attack." ICMP (Internet Control Messaging Protocol) "pings" other devices on a network as a way of checking on their online status. When a targeted server receives too many pings, as in various high-profile attacks on Amazon.com and other companies, the server is overwhelmed in its efforts to respond to the multitude of ICMP messages.

In addition to hacker attacks, some policies also provide coverage against credit card fraud. Although not yet widely available, that kind of insurance is likely to become quite appealing to e-businesses. "Fraud is much more real and tangible than hackers," according to Alan Fisher, cofounder of OnSale.com. OnSale, says Fisher, "gets hit by orchestrated fraud rings about two to four times a year. Professional theft rings typically steal $25,000 to $100,000 worth of merchandise each time."

You can also protect yourself from fraud by hiring a screening service such as Internet Billing Company (www.ibill.com). The company scores credit card transactions according to their fraud potential. E-mail addresses are checked for accuracy, as are street addresses. According to a recent *Fortune* article on ibill.com, "The company also

Red Flags for E-Fraud

WATCH OUT FOR the following signs of credit card fraud on the Web. A single one shouldn't be a cause of alarm, says Visa USA, but if several occur at one time, be sure to investigate before you complete the transaction.

1 **Larger-than-normal orders.** The customer may be using stolen cards or phony account numbers that have a limited life span. If the customer is looking to conduct fraudulent transactions, he needs to maximize the size of his purchase.

2 **Orders for multiples of the same item.** If a crook intends to resell them, having more will increase profits.

3 **Orders made up of big-ticket items.** These have maximum resale value and maximum profit potential.

4 **Orders shipped "rush" or overnight.** This person wants the fraudulently obtained items in his hands as soon as possible for the quickest resale—extra delivery charges aren't a concern.

makes use of extensive databases with information on problem or fraudulent cards."

Internet scams are pervasive and increasingly shrewd. To begin to avoid them, you can make use of the several technologies described here and in Appendix A. But of even greater importance than technology for defeating scam artists is your vigilance and common sense. Anyone who needs an immediate answer to a "bargain offer," who requires a credit card number as a sign of good faith, or who cannot provide bona fide business identification (address, credit history, and so on) is certainly to be avoided.

Summing Up Step 6

IN THE SAME WAY THAT A DEPARTMENT STORE ERECTS SENSOR panels at its exits to prevent merchandise theft, so you as an e-business owner must be extremely careful to protect your best ideas, programming secrets, logos and labels, business contacts, customer names, and operational processes. Legal measures such as patents and copyrights can provide part of this protection. But you must also work with your entire team to keep the competition guessing "How do they do it?" In addition, you must be vigilant that scams are not perpetrated on or by your company. Your security efforts will go far to preserving the uniqueness and competitive advantage of your e-business concept.

7

STEP 7

Build a Fast, Functional Web Site

IN TURNING TO THE DESIGN OF YOUR WEB site, you may feel somewhat overwhelmed by the hundreds of thousands of different Web page layouts now on the Internet, with more arriving at a rate of about 10,000 per week. Getting ideas for your site is the easy part; getting your head straight on which ideas belong in your site is the hard part.

So take it a step at a time. You have already assembled a business plan that defines the purpose of your site, locates your intended marketplace, and tells how you will do business. Your goal in shaping your Web site is to "let form follow function"—that is, wrap the design of your site around what it is supposed to do.

This chapter deals with Web site design for both business-to-consumer (B2C) and business-to-business (B2B) Web sites. Because the latter are usually industry specific in their design criteria, a reputable industry Web site designer is usually required for the creation and maintenance of B2B Web sites. The general principles of Web site design offered here, however, will guide both those who are involved in developing their own Web sites and those who are working with a commercial site designer.

You're Not Late to the Game

FROM THE VERY BEGINNING, TRY TO REASSURE YOURself that you have not waited too long to join the e-business revolution. Remember that in 2000 only about one in seven small businesses were conducting commerce on the Web. Recall as well that in 2000 less than 0.5 percent of retail spending took place on the Web. You're not late to the game.

Aside from the pressures of your own financial goals, there's no reason to rush the design stage of your Web site (as too many entrepreneurs have, to their regret). Set what you consider a reasonable timetable for producing a first-class site, then be patient with yourself as you encounter the infamous learning curve along the way. A well-designed site that comes along somewhat slowly is infinitely preferable to a slapdash, rush-to-market site that will cause endless headaches for you and your customers.

The Components of a Great E-Business Web Site

NO SERIOUS ARTIST PAINTS BY THE NUMBERS, AND THE STEPS that follow are not intended as a rigid forced march for the production of your site. Surely you will hop back and forth among these steps as your site takes shape. Some rational order, however, can provide a useful starting place for the great business adventure that lies ahead.

First, choose the right domain name. Don't you wish you had been the person to think of unforgettable names such as Kleenex, Spaghettios, Kibbles 'N Bits, Frosted Flakes—or, for that matter, Citicorp, Allstate, Prudential, AutoDesk, and Apple? You now have that opportunity: your domain name is the moniker you will use most often in referring to your e-business and, we hope, will be the name that sticks in the minds of your customers.

As you probably know, a domain name is the word that comes just before the dot in your Web address. For millions of Americans, "aol" is their domain in such user names as susan@aol.com. You could do business, of course, as "spoons@prodigy.net" or "forks@mindspring.com." Virtually every e-business site designer, however, will counsel against this option for those setting up e-business sites.

Here are four reasons why you will probably want your own domain name. First, you may end up spending more money when you rely on another party's domain name (as in toys@compuserve.com). Wherever your domain holder goes in terms of increased fees, accessibility, use or lack of new technologies, and so forth, there you must follow. Take away the "compuserve.com" from your e-business and you're just "toys," twisting in the cyber-wind. With your own domain name, you can switch hosts (more about hosts soon) at will. In short, your e-business is mobile with its own domain name.

Second, your own domain name (such as toys.com—don't think about it, the name's been taken!) gives you exclusivity. No one else among the many millions of Web users can legitimately use your domain name. Third, it confers a certain credibility, much as in bricks-and-mortar businesses the "Inc." tag-on signals a serious business enterprise. Finally, you won't get caught in the name-changing dilemma, with consequent loss of market momentum. Your name, which you've worked hard to ingrain in the public mind, never has to be changed—nor does your business card.

QUALITIES OF A GREAT DOMAIN NAME

AS WITH NAMING CHILDREN-TO-BE, THE FIRST NAME THAT pops into your head may not be the one you settle on for the long term. Take some time, therefore, to make sure your domain name has at least three things going for it:

1 **The name should be easy to remember and convey.** You're going to be saying your domain name thousands of times to customers ("Check out my products at...") and placing it on business stationery, cards, advertising, products, T-shirts, and perhaps your license plate as well. So make sure that the name is uncomplicated yet memorable. There's no shame in asking trustworthy friends to help out in this name game, as long as they don't send a bill for services rendered or claim a piece of your business action.

2 **The name should not be easily misspelled or confused with a more well-known name.** You gain nothing but problems, legal and otherwise, by calling yourself "beakins-moving.com" or "aplecomputer.com." Nor should you use separation marks such as hyphens and underscores, which your customers will confuse endlessly. (Can you imagine yourself saying on the telephone for the umpteenth time, "No, it's with an underscore, not a hyphen"?)

3 **The name should fit your e-business like a glove, not a strait-jacket.** If you sell fertilizers for houseplants, your

first inclination might be to opt for a domain name such as "greenleaves.com" (and yes, it's probably already taken, too!). But when your business expands into pots, greenhouse shelving, watering systems, and so forth, you may wish that you had chosen a less restrictive domain name. Although a name cannot suggest every product or service in your line, it should not limit your customers' impressions of your operation.

GETTING YOUR DOMAIN NAME

AFTER YOU'VE FOUND YOUR IDEAL NAME, THINK OF AT LEAST ten that you like just as well. Why? You will undoubtedly find that many of your favorite domain names have already been taken by others. (If you absolutely must have a certain name, check sites that sell names others have registered, including Greatname.com. Be prepared to spend some money, however. Some quite catchy and desirable names have sold in the six figures, with a few in the seven figures.)

Armed with your list of possible domain names, go to internic.net to see which are still available. About 100,000 domain names per month are now being registered, so time is of the essence in getting a name that serves you well. There are now several sites where you can register your domain name as exclusively yours for a period of two years. At the end of the two years you may renew the name ad infinitum. One of the most experienced among such registry sites is netsolutions.com. You'll pay about $150 for registry services and receive confirmation of your domain name by both e-mail and regular mail. Congratulations! You're now heyihaveadomainname.com.

FOCUSING ON YOUR CUSTOMERS' NEEDS

BEGIN TO PLAN YOUR WEB SITE FROM YOUR CUSTOMERS' POINT of view. If you were a busy client on an especially hassled day, what would (and wouldn't) you like to see when you clicked to the Web site we're now discussing? In surveys of just such creatures, here is the common litany of Likes and Dislikes:

CUSTOMERS LIKE . . .

- **fast loading.** Any loading longer than five seconds becomes frustrating.
- **clear orientation.** What site is this, what can I do here, how does it work?
- **professional, creative flair.** Black boxes on a white screen look like a Gulag cell. Although customers don't want or expect a cornucopia of sights and sounds, they do expect a sharp-looking Web site reflecting your customer-friendly attitude.
- **easy navigation.** How do I get from the introduction page to the order page? How do I get back? Can I see at a glance the kinds of pages that are available to me at this site?
- **contact information.** If I have a problem or question, how do I get in touch?
- **useful links.** In considering my purchasing options, I may need to scrounge around the Web for some information. It's nice when links to those usual sources of information are provided right at the site. For example, someone buying clothing for an international trip may want to check out temperatures in Madrid or London. A trumpet player looking over your horns for sale may want to link quickly to the American Trumpet Association for some general information or specific details.
- **good balance between rich content and comfortable display.** Customers don't mind a Web page that is chock-full of useful links and items, so long as those bits of text and graphics are displayed in a well-organized, appealing way. Take a look, for example, at the home pages for Yahoo!, AOL, MSN, Netscape, or other service providers. Those pages are full to the bursting point with information and icons of all kinds, but in general they are arranged well for ease of perception and ease of use.

CUSTOMERS DISLIKE . . .

- **slow-loading graphics,** especially when those pictures add little or nothing to the usefulness of the site.
- **tricky sites that won't let you return easily to your browser.** Although your author is entirely innocent of such

things, it is whispered that many porn sites are programmed in such a way that you can't exit the miserable things by the usual ways. Some mainstream e-business sites have begun to imitate this annoying practice. Customers sometimes find that they have to completely shut down their computers to once and for all get away from a URL that just won't die.

- **sites that contain no road map to their contents.** Customers do not want to explore your site pages to see how they relate to one another. From your first page, it should be abundantly clear how to navigate around the contents of your site. As a test in this regard, see if someone new to your site can understand how to navigate its pages within the first five seconds of looking at your first page. If not, redesign it for easier use.
- **features that exist only in an effort to show off the programmer's skill.** So Mount Vesuvius erupts at your Web site and your products surf down on the bright red lava? This might win a programming award, but it can also drive customers away. Clever graphics and animations are fine as long as they do not retard or interrupt the business purpose of your site. Here's the rubric: everything on the Web page is intended to serve the customer's convenience and interests.

OTHER HINTS FOR A WINNING DESIGN

HERE ARE SEVEN ADDITIONAL IDEAS TO CONSIDER IN DESIGNing a fully integrated, effective, and visually pleasing Web site that customers can navigate with ease:

1 **Remember that not all customers enter through the front door or first page of your site.** Many will bookmark interior pages of your site and go directly there for shopping or other business. Your contact information (including company name, click-through to an e-mail screen, and perhaps your fax, phone, and street address, if appropriate) should appear on every page of your site.

2 **All colors should coordinate.** You probably have worked diligently to see that foreground, background, font, and other colors work well together. But the often-forgotten color that stands out like a sore thumb is the hyperlink color setting. Make sure that it, too, contributes to a pleasing view.

3 **Add a feedback form to your site.** Even if only one out of a hundred customers actually takes the time to use it, many of those hundred will be favorably impressed that your company seeks out and listens to customer input. The feedback form, of course, should not be merely for show. Make sure that someone in your organization responds quickly to any feedback received.

4 **A picture is still worth a thousand words, but choose your graphics with great care.** Don't assume, for example, that all purchasing agents for auto tools will appreciate a buxom lass in a bikini holding a torque wrench as a highlight on your home page. If your graphics are wonderful but s-l-o-w in coming up onscreen, there are several free services you can use to compress these graphic files for quick downloading. One such service is located at www.webutilities.com/services/index.htm.

5 **Consider adding a search function to your home page** so that customers don't have to scan through several pages looking for the Beanie Baby with the plaid shorts. If you've chosen to do your own programming (discussed a bit later in this chapter), you may want to experiment with Microsoft Front Page, which makes it quite easy to insert search tools into your site.

6 **Let customers know when your site was last updated.** Product descriptions and service terms inevitably change over time. No customer likes to find out late in the transaction that the Web site incorrectly described prices, dimensions, availability, shipping arrangements, and so forth. You can simply indicate (usually at the bottom of your home page) the date when the site was last updated. You can also include a "What's New for Today" or "What's New This Week" page that you update more regularly than the rest of the site. If your pricing tends to change more often than your product or service descriptions, it may be most practical to handle prices on a "Click for Current Price Information" basis.

7 **Do your customers the favor of adding a "Helpful Links" page to your site.** Because you know your business, you can predict what other sites your customers will

probably frequent (or should learn to use, if they are new to your area of business). These sites can include associations, trade groups, university sites, government information centers, and many others. Be sure to visit these sites yourself on a regular basis to make sure you are not steering your customers to a dead link (which reflects poorly on you) or a site that has lost its usefulness. Especially when dealing with other e-businesses, it's common courtesy to request permission to link their site to yours. If you wish, you can request that they do likewise. Building this kind of referral network can be extremely valuable in developing and extending your client base.

The Big Decision: To Outsource Site Development or Do It Yourself

IN THIS MOST IMPORTANT DISCUSSION, LET'S ASSUME FROM the outset that you do not have a whiz-kid nephew or niece who is willing to hold your hand through the development and maintenance of your do-it-yourself Web site. (If you have such a kid around, good for you—read the next section on outsourcing, which is in fact what you're doing via this youngster, whether paid or not.)

Not long ago your only realistic hope of creating an attractive Web page on your own involved learning the intricacies of HTML, the programming language of the World Wide Web. Sure, you could learn HTML, but you probably don't have time. You have an e-business to develop! Fortunately, we now have a wide variety of writing and editing tools that make it unnecessary for you to learn a programming language per se.

Here's why you might consider creating and maintaining your own Web site. First, you will save money in both the short and the long term. Web site developers and consultants (and there are scads to choose from in every area of the country) typically get $100 to $150 per hour, including prolonged conversation sessions in which they try to get to know your business, customers, products, and services. It's not unusual for a small-scale e-business to pay $5,000 to

$10,000 to such a developer before seeing anything resembling a Web site actually appear on the Internet. (This is not said to disparage the skills or work of Web site developers and designers. In my experience, they are highly proficient and usually earn their keep.) Add to this start-up investment the regular payments you will make to the developer or another skilled person to maintain your site, update it, and fix the inevitable glitches. If a professional Web site designer puts your site together, it's unlikely that you will be able to maintain it yourself. As with fine watches, the general rule is this: the more expensive the creation, the more you will require specialized help for maintenance. Have you serviced your Rolex yourself lately?

The most credible source for do-it-yourself advice is a person who has created an ambitious Web site for his company—namely, Kenneth E. Johnson, training and support manager at the law firm of Mayer, Brown & Platt in Chicago. Here's his succinct, nuts-and-bolts description of how to go about fashioning your own Web site:

- **You don't have to be an HTML guru;** you can create Web pages from programs as widely used as Microsoft Word 6.0 and WordPerfect 6.1 for Windows. Both programs have HTML add-ons that let you create, with the help of special toolbars and menu commands, Web pages as Word or WordPerfect documents. With a couple of mouse clicks, you can export the document in HTML format. It should now be ready for posting on the Web. The vast majority of formatting can be accomplished without ever entering an HTML tag.
- **Word users can choose Microsoft's Internet Assistant** (downloadable for free at www.microsoft.com) **or Quarterdeck's WebAuthor** ($49 retail). Internet Assistant not only adds HTML editing capability but also turns Word into a minimal Web browser. WebAuthor provides a button bar and dialog boxes for all HTML tags and validates HTML code. WebAuthor also has a very powerful forms-creation feature.
- **WordPerfect 6.1 users can obtain Novell's Internet Publisher free of charge** at www.novell.com. Internet Publisher includes not only the WP6.1 HTML template but also the Netscape Web browser and Envoy document viewer.

So you can easily obtain the technical skill for Web page creation. But what about the design skill? Though this takes a little more work, it's not difficult. There are many resources available that discuss design points. HTML books and resources on the Web are good places to begin your research (for example, see the "Style Guide for On-line Hypertext" available at http://info.cern.ch/hypertext/WWW/Provider/Style/Overview.html).

The Other Side of the Street: Hiring a Professional Web Site Designer

LET'S BE FRANK ABOUT THE REASONS WHY YOU MAY WANT TO spend the money for a professional Web site designer. It has nothing to do with smarts: of course you could take the time to develop your own site, but then you could also learn to repair your car's transmission and rewire your house. For most of us, it comes down to a question of time and energy. Every moment you spend trying to figure out a sticky wicket in your Web site programming is a moment away from activities that probably will turn out to be more profitable. These include thinking hard about your e-business strategy, learning about your competition, extending your network of e-business associates and acquaintances, talking to people who may be interested in working for you, developing winning marketing approaches, and so forth. These activities are the core business of entrepreneurs and can't be set aside for a technical hobby.

In addition, your do-it-yourself efforts will probably run into more than one shoal along the way. You'll discover that different browsers display the same HTML information very differently. The Web site you design under AOL may not work well when viewed through Netscape. The graphics that load so quickly for you in a DSL environment turn out to be at least ten times slower for those using traditional telephone modem connections.

Then there's the matter of finding the right server to host your fledgling Web site. In transferring your files to the chosen server, what professionals can do in two minutes may take you several hours—the dreaded learning curve again. There's also the matter of maintenance and repair to consider. Although you were able to put together a Web site that runs passably well, are you equally prepared to get back into it for updates and repairs?

Finally, think about the best of all possible scenarios: your e-business concept takes off as you never expected, and you find yourself swamped by inquiries and orders. A professional Web designer will plan for such success by making your Web site "scalable," that is, easily adjustable to increased levels of traffic. Your own efforts may not have built in this kind of flexibility for your site.

CHOOSING A WEB DESIGNER

THE PROCESS OF CHOOSING A WEB DESIGNER IS A BIT LIKE choosing a spouse: you want to meet lots of prospects before you choose, you want to observe the selected one carefully, and it's nice if he or she is local.

Begin your search for the right Web site designer by keying in the search words "Web designers." AOL Search produced no fewer than 9,000 hits for services all around the world ready to assist you in your development efforts. In paring down that list to something reasonable, here are recommended selection criteria:

1 **Choose an experienced Web design firm that can point you to many of their previous projects.** Take time to visit these sites to see if you like the concept and workmanship. Above all, look at the designers' own Web pages. Certainly the designers can't do for you what they weren't able to do for themselves on the Web.
2 **If possible, choose a Web designer you can visit in person.** Sharing your background, goals, strategies, and business plans is much easier in person than by e-mail or telephone.
3 **Don't rush to get a firm price.** The designer has a right to know what's entailed in your e-business before quoting numbers. Do, however, settle on firm financial arrangements in writing before work begins. If you are worried that an hourly arrangement might run in the direction of the

national debt, include in your contract a "not to exceed" clause that specifies the maximum you will have to pay, no matter what the expense of time in hours.

4 **Listen well and ask for suggestions.** You are hiring expertise, after all, not just a robot to carry out your vision of a Web site. There's an excellent chance that the professional you select will offer ideas you haven't thought of.

5 **Select a designer with whom you share good interpersonal feelings.** The last thing you need in the heat of a Web site meltdown is a moody designer who doesn't like your attitude.

6 **Structure payments in a series of stages.** A designer will probably show you a Web site "shell" (basic layout, foreground and background colors and textures, and so on) for your approval before working on more detailed features. Each of these stages toward completion can be used as a pay period.

7 **Let the designer know your budget.** Large companies such as Levi's and Sears invested millions of dollars in Web site development. Your designer will scale his or her range of creative options to the approximate money you have available.

8 **Discuss ongoing maintenance and update services with your designer.** This is often their least-favorite part of the job, but you will want to be sure that someone can maintain and fix the shining new site you're driving out of the dealership.

9 **Ask for the designer's advice regarding hosting services.** He or she has probably had many experiences, good and bad, with various Web site hosts. You don't have to repeat that trail of learning to make a wise decision about a host for your site.

10 **Don't let the designer, for all his or her insight and skill, roll over your desires** for how you want your Web site to look and work. Like interior home designers, some very talented Web site designers have a tendency to forget that you, not they, will be "living" in this site and doing business there. Make sure the result you're paying for pleases you.

Finding the Right Host for Your Web Site

UNTIL YOUR FILES ARE "HOSTED," THEY CANNOT BE SAID TO constitute a Web site at all. You could, of course, invest the $100,000 or so it conservatively takes to purchase, program, install, and maintain your own server linked directly to an Internet hub in a major city near you. For most small and midsized businesses, that is not practical. Instead, you, like 95 percent of all e-business owners, will pay a hosting company a monthly fee to keep your Web site on the Internet.

But before you write your check, you should at least explore some of the 200 or so Web hosting companies that offer their services for free. They will ask that you bring your site to them in completed form (whether by do-it-yourself efforts or the work of a professional designer). They will then provide the necessary expertise in getting your Web site up and running on the Internet. Most Internet service providers make this "free home page" available as part of their bundled services and include it in the monthly fee. Services such as Geocities and Excite also offer a free home page.

But here's the rub: these "free" home pages for your Web site make their money by allowing advertisers to pop up in the banner area of your site, often every minute or so. You have little or no control over who advertises at your site; the classic story tells about the exterminator's ads placed on a site selling ant farms. Your customers may quickly tire of the barrage of unrelated advertising they must endure to do business at your site.

In addition, these free services typically provide no support, technical or otherwise, if you experience problems with your site. They make no guarantees about the quality of the hosting service and have little flexibility if you want to install more sophisticated software for attaching orders to inventory control, processing payments, and so forth.

It would be a shame to see a wonderfully developed Web site poorly hosted and ill served, even though for free. Therefore, the vast majority of small-business owners have decided to pay the $50 to $100 per month for standard Web site hosting services. One free online service that will help you get to know and compare the various hosting services available is TopHosts.com. Its database contains all the necessary details about hundreds of companies providing hosting services. Drawn from that database, the following table presents a typical array of price and function options among hosting packages.

SERVICE/FEATURE	ENTRY-LEVEL	STANDARD	PREMIUM
Setup Fee	$50	$200	$500
Domain Name	One	Multiple	Multiple
Disk Space	20Mb	75Mb	1G
Data Transfer	1G	5G	50G
Other Services	E-Mail	E-Mail, Store	E-Mail, Store
Monthly Fee	$20–$50	$50–$250	$250–$1,000

Summing Up Step 7

WITH A FEW HOURS OF READING, INTERNET SURFING, AND experimenting, you will find that a modest Internet presence, complete with Visa and MasterCard capability, is certainly within your range of skill. The question remains, however, whether such a site is in your best interest. If your e-business idea proves its worth and customer contacts begin flowing in, your homemade or off-the-shelf site may quickly prove to be too limited for your number of hits and too expensive, in terms of fees to others, for a sustainable enterprise. Think seriously, therefore, about involving the talent of a reputable Web site designer from the beginning of your e-business project. Much like an architect, this person will help you make sense out of your various programming options so that the electronic house of business you eventually create will be useful, durable, attractive, and expandable.

At the same time, remember that designing a Web site that fits your business purpose is part science and part art. Your research into site design and your counsel with site design experts is the science part. But there always remains room for that special, even risky personal touch that makes the site interesting, human, and uniquely yours. Give your imagination free rein and take that risk. Nothing is cast in granite in Web site programming. You can always remove and repair a misstep. Hold open the hope that your imaginative touches to your Web site won't turn out to be missteps at all, but rather giant leaps forward.

8

STEP 8

Market Your E-Business

HERE'S THE BAD NEWS: WITHOUT significant work on your part, the chances that potential customers will find your Web site on the Internet are less than finding the proverbial needle in the haystack. But the flip side is the good news: you have it entirely within your power to draw thousands of hits to your Web site per month, and eventually per week or per day.

Although many of the marketing techniques treated here apply equally to business-to-consumer and business-to-business companies, the latter may also encounter marketing challenges beyond the scope of this book. Specifically, business-to-business enterprises involved in trading associations such as MetalSiteLP, Chemdex, General Electric's GEIS site, or Ingersoll-Rand's Lightning Manufacturing Project (see Step 9) will find built-in marketing channels within the highly sophisticated software for these business groups. The intent of this chapter is not to show a chemical manufacturer, for example, how to use Chemdex software to do business within that group but instead to discuss the broader question of how an e-business outside the circle of an industry group can market itself successfully.

Looking beyond Banner Ads

WHEN YOU THINK OF INTERNET ADVERTISING, YOU probably think first of the ubiquitous banner ads that flutter across the top of your screen or, when you first sign in to your Web browser, force you to click a very little box saying "No Thanks" before you can proceed with your business or surfing. This chapter will show you how to use such banner ads inexpensively or for free. The chapter will also try to persuade you to look beyond banner advertising for more effective ways to attract and hold customers.

SO WHAT'S WRONG WITH BANNER ADS?

LET'S NOT DRAW CONCLUSIONS ABOUT BANNER ADS BASED ON the fact that more than 80 percent of the space intended for banner advertising goes unsold each day, or that rates for banner advertising have steadily plummeted in the past several years. Instead, consider your own experience with banner advertising.

First, have you ever purchased anything based on a banner ad? If so, analyze what it was about the ad or product description that won your attention and patronage. Have you ever even clicked through to explore what a banner ad was advertising? Many of the most intense Internet users (those online more than 40 hours per week) admit that they have never purchased anything from a banner ad. Some say that they would not purchase through this medium because they consider banner ads an annoyance.

Originally, planners at Yahoo!, AOL, Prodigy, and other prominent Internet service providers (ISPs) projected that banner advertising on the Internet would follow about the same pattern as television or radio advertising. Supposedly, a Web site could use counters and other measurements to demonstrate a certain number of viewers. It could then compute a CPM (cost per thousand) to charge anyone who wished to place a banner advertisement to be seen by visitors to that Web site. Yahoo!, for example, charges $20 to $50 for each 1,000 "views" of a banner ad placed on one of its pages. Obviously, home pages of ISPs are the most expensive, with interior pages costing significantly less. Think about the expense, however, for a single banner ad: letting 100,000 people have a glimpse of your banner ad (and a glimpse is certainly all that most of us give to such ads) could easily cost you $5,000, not including production expenses for the ad itself. Many prominent sites attract that kind of traffic in less than an hour.

Why has banner advertising been a bust at a period when television, radio, and print advertising has soared both in volume and in profitability? First, banner ads have little to recommend them to the eye or mind. They usually aren't beautiful, funny, moving, or clever. Second, we are never forced to view them (as we are to some degree forced to look at the TV screen during a commercial break); we can always look instead at the rest of the screen, the portion that attracted our interest in the first place. Finally, they have been tainted (often unjustly) with a reputation for hucksterism. We usually have no idea with whom we're dealing when we decide to click through on a banner ad. We typically do not see the superstars of American business advertising their products in banner ads. We conclude, rightly or wrongly, that such ads will take us to a flea market of low-quality goods and services.

For these reasons and others, less than 0.5 percent of the American advertising dollar was spent on Internet advertising in 2000. Although total numbers of Internet users were expected to triple from 1999 levels by the end of 2002, no serious advertising analyst has expected Internet advertising revenues to follow that same curve or even approach it. Some analysts predict the drop in rates for CPM Internet advertising will continue as more and more business Web sites lower their advertising rates in a desperate effort to fill even a small portion of their available advertising space.

Ten Marketing Techniques beyond Banner Advertising

BEFORE RELYING PRIMARILY ON BANNER ADVERTISING TO spread the word about your excellent products or services, give thought to using most or all of the following advertising approaches. You will find that they cost far less than banners and usually bring superior results. You will also find that these approaches take more sustained effort on your part—which probably explains why they are not as popular as placing banner ads.

1 **Barter an exchange of advertising links with associated (but not directly competitive) companies.** Say you sell collectible plates and another Web site sells display cabinets. It's in both of your interests to let customers know about both your businesses. To get the process started, e-mail the business owner with a sincere, fully developed

description of who you are and what your business is. Emphasize what your site could provide to link customers to the other person's business, and then suggest what similar links you would request in return. You may want to suggest a short trial period—thirty days is typical—to determine if both parties are happy with the arrangement. Usually no money changes hands in this quid pro quo advertising arrangement. In establishing such partnerships, you will often find many other businesses that can be brought into your shared advertising arrangement. Someone, for example, makes hardware such as drawer pulls and hinges for the display cabinets. Another business may provide you with preferential packing and shipping charges. All these merchants, service providers, or manufacturers are good candidates for advertising exchanges that cost you nothing more than your time.

2 **Become involved in a link exchange.** The concept works like this: every entrepreneur or small- to medium-sized-business owner faces the dilemma of placing ads on a limited budget. If all these owners got together and agreed to allow one another to advertise on each other's Web sites without charge, a "win-win" situation would emerge from what otherwise was a total loss. Several organizations have arisen to provide just this linkage. The most prominent of these is www.linkexchange.com, which claims to have about 200,000 businesses exchanging advertising space on a gratis basis. Check it out.

3 **Become known within a newsgroup.** Note that I did not say advertise to a newsgroup (a self-organized set of Internet users, who often resent outside intrusion). Many of these special interest groups have a powerful bias against unsolicited advertising—so powerful, in fact, that you may find your e-mail jammed for weeks if you offend a newsgroup by cramming your advertisements into its cyberspace. Better to join the newsgroup and let it emerge naturally that you are "in the business" and can provide excellent prices for desirable products and services. You'll find that many others within the newsgroup are also there for the potential business, not just for chat. As with many aspects of advertising, timing

and presentation are all. Don't step into the territory of an established newsgroup in a clumsy way. Enter politely through the front door as a new member and become acquainted before you sell your wares.

There are now well over 300,000 newsgroups of all types and purposes on the Internet. Surely more than one fits your customer profile (and if not, you may want to examine your profile!). The best way to locate newsgroups in line with your business interests is to scan the list (the long list) at www.reference.com, which at this writing included information on more than 150,000 newsgroups.

4 **Solicit business on a one-to-one basis through well-placed e-mail messages.** Promotional e-mail messages no doubt arrive on your screen almost every day, as they do on mine. As a general rule, the ones we delete without reading even a single word are those that appear impersonal, insincere, overhyped, overly familiar, or flimflammish ("Buy a house without spending a dime!" and so on). If you choose to pursue an e-mail promotional campaign, keep four guidelines in mind when constructing your messages:

◆ *Get right to the point about what your business offers from the customer's point of view.* Do you offer name-brand fishing equipment at 25 percent off typical prices in sports stores? Say so up front! Can you provide watch repair on a 48-hour turnaround instead of the weeks most watch repair shops require? Let your customer know right away. This customer-focused "hook" is infinitely more successful in producing sales than hucksterish come-ons and attempts at humor.

◆ *Keep your message very brief, with a click-through option if the reader would like more information.* Bear in mind, however, that the popular browsers handle hypertext URLs within e-mail messages quite differently. Your reader may not be able to click on your URL within your message simply because the reader's browser does not present it as hypertext. It's important, therefore, to give a brief URL (www.watches.com versus www.wesellwatcheswholesale.com) in case your reader ends up having to key it in.

◆ *Make sure your message contains a specific statement of what you would like the reader to do.* Virtually all research on direct mail and e-mail solicitation shows that readers tend to do what they are specifically told to do. Do you want your reader to contact you for a free sample? Tell exactly how the reader should do so. Do you want to give the reader a bid of some kind? Tell precisely what specifications or other information you will require for an accurate bid.

◆ *Finally, conclude your message with friendly reassurance about your business policies and general attitude.* The reader, after all, does not know you from Adam or Eve. Such phrases as "We stand behind our work," "We provide a one-year customer satisfaction guarantee," "We are known for expert, honest work," and so forth build the reader's confidence in doing business with you. If you have space within your short message, you may also want to include testimonials from satisfied customers and/or company names on your client list. (Be sure to get permission, of course, before using such testimonials or names in your advertising.)

You can gain access to mailing lists from many Web companies (use the search words "mailing list" to see dozens of these). One highly regarded company of this sort is www.liszt.com, which has available more than 100,000 mailing lists. Remember, however, that e-mail advertising flows not only from you to the potential customer but from the customer to you as well. Gear up for handling a potentially massive response from your extensive e-mail marketing campaign. Those who contact you are understandably unwilling to wait several days to hear back from you.

Your business e-mail system may not yet be set up to handle success in the form of hundreds or thousands of e-mails to you in a single day. Make sure your system can handle such crucial functions as the following:

◆ **Autoresponse.** This is a message that automatically goes out as a response immediately upon receiving an e-mail. The message may simply say, "Thank you very much for your interest in our Internet offer. The positive response has been overwhelming, and we are working as fast as we can to fill orders as they were received. We will be getting back to you within the next 24 hours. We appreciate your patience." The point is that you let the customer know that you're on top of things at your business and that you appreciate the reader's contact.

Both small-business entrepreneurs and larger businesses with Web sites can distinguish themselves for quality of operations and concern for customer satisfaction by simply getting back quickly to e-mail contacts. Even a mere acknowledgment that the customer's e-mail has been received and will be answered soon (as in the example above) is preferable to the Big Chill of no answer at all.

◆ **A mailing-list builder.** Many people will contact you to give you a different e-mail address than the one you used in your original contact, or to give you e-mail addresses of other people you should contact. Make sure you can collect these into a well-organized address book that easily becomes your mailing list for future contacts.

◆ **Signature files.** Your company information, including company name, your name and title, your URL, and (if you wish) other contact information such as fax or phone numbers, should appear in a standard signature file that is automatically added to the end of each e-mail. You can also include company slogans, disclosure or licensing information, and other brief phrases in your "sig file." A signature file should also contain specific information on how an e-mail recipient can opt out of receiving future e-mails from the company or be dropped from a mailing list.

These are not exotic functions that require investment in new software. Such familiar systems as Outlook Express and Netscape Messenger already include them.

5 **Advertise your products or services by becoming an indispensable information source or newsletter publisher.** Let's say, for example, that you specialize in buying and selling used musical instruments, especially trumpets and trombones. One way to dramatically increase traffic to your Web site is to simply list serial numbers or other identifying data along with the year of manufacture for a variety of instruments. Web users who don't think they are in the market for buying or selling an instrument may come to your site simply to see when their instrument was made. If your site is shrewdly constructed, they will be ushered seamlessly

from their information gathering to your showcase of available instruments. This technique for attracting Web traffic has worked for thousands of sites, including those providing maps, names of embassies, telephone listings for many cities, currency conversion, census information, facts on file, and a multitude of other desired forms of information.

A variant of this plan is to generate an information-packed newsletter for your target audience of customers. This publication need not be long. In fact, for e-mailing purposes, you will probably want to keep it to 25K to 30K or so. Most readers probably will not read more, and a long newsletter can cause problems in electronic distribution. (You can imagine the server problems involved if many business owners on the same ISP each decided to send out a long newsletter to 15,000 subscribers on the same day.)

The newsletter contains your expertise in the form of tips, contacts, information, regulations, product information, trade association names, and so forth. You probably can put the touch on a few friends to write occasional guest columns. Q & A columns featuring questions from subscribers seem especially popular (the "Ann Landers" approach to marketing success). Like any good journalist, you should maintain a clear separation between what's news and what's advertising. If you're talking about new EPA guidelines for outdoor house paint, for example, don't muddy the waters in the same article by telling how your products meet all those guidelines. Let a nearby ad do that work for you.

Subscribers don't want to feel that your news is just a diving board to your advertising. I use the word "subscriber" rather loosely, because the vast majority of newsletters are sent for free. In fact, your subscribers should know your policy in advance for selling their names, addresses, and other information to other marketers. Nothing unravels good customer relations more quickly than having new customers receive a spate of junk e-mail simply because they did business with you.

How often should you publish your newsletter? That depends on your available time, energy, and talent. Except in time-sensitive environments such as financial investments, a newsletter that comes out weekly is probably too much of a good thing and often goes unread. On average, newsletters that have sustained their audience for a year or more tend to come out monthly. If you wait much longer than that between issues, you risk a falloff in reader interest and loyalty.

The nuts-and-bolts task of becoming an electronic publisher of your own newsletter can be daunting, especially at first, during your learning-curve and getting-organized period. If you want help with maintaining your mailing list (the primary complaint of overworked newsletter publishers), you may want to subcontract the work to one of several companies specializing in such services. These include www.skylist.net/hosting and www.lyris.net.

6 **List your business with a number of search engines.** Can't the search engine find you without your help? Of course—but much more slowly and unpredictably than if you enter your company name, information, and URL directly with the search engine. The process is straightforward for almost all major search engine sites. Go to the site, seek the "add a page" or "add URL" button (sometimes accessible via the Help option), then follow the on-screen instructions for adding your information to the search engine listings.

After you have accomplished such registration, you may be frustrated that your company name doesn't come up at the top of the heap when a typical search phrase for your line of business is keyed in (such as "carpet repair"). The fact that you are listed 400th instead of 1st in the listings that come back from the search has nothing to do with the size of your business, its newness on the Internet, or someone else's payoffs to the people who run the search engine. It is useful, of course, for your business to come up near the top of the list whenever possible. Increasing your chances for such placement involves some technical manipulation of your site, including "meta-tags," that isn't within the scope of this book. But you can get more information on how to appear earlier rather than later in a search list by contacting companies specializing in such consultation, such as www.positions.com.

7 **Join a mall.** In the bricks-and-mortar Old Economy, stores often choose to locate in a mall because they share a great

deal of traffic there with other stores. These stores all pay rent, of course, as you will if you join an online mall. The question is whether you will enjoy increased traffic to your site as a result of joining an electronic mall.

On the positive side, it can be shown statistically that a large traffic flow comes to the "front door" or home page of the mall—and many malls sell their rental space based primarily on these home page visitor counts. But unlike a bricks-and-mortar mall, where customers have to pass dozens of shopwindows on their way to the merchant of their choice, the online mall allows shoppers to go straight to their buying destination without passing your shop at all. At best, customers have seen only the name of your shop listed with dozens (or hundreds) of others at the main portal to the online mall. At worst, customers never see your site or learn about any of your products, services, or special offers unless those customers key in a search word that takes them right to your door. In the case of larger online malls, thousands of merchants lie electronically hidden within the mall software. A broad search word such as "wallpaper" may turn up a hundred or more shopping sources. This is said not to discourage you from considering mall membership but just to prepare you for the realities of what you may encounter there. You won't feel like Macy's.

Some of the most prominent online malls are Yahoo! Store (www.yahoo.com), Downtown Anywhere (www.awa.com), the Internet Mall (www.internet-mall.com), and iCat (www.icatmall.com). The fees charged for mall membership vary, but they usually are based on the number of items you plan to advertise through the site as well as the volume of your business.

8 Internationalize your site for a global customer base. Although most Web users are Americans, the largest percentage gains in new Web users in the next three years is expected to come from abroad. Imagine, for example, when even a small percentage of China's or India's huge populations are linked to the Internet for the first time.

You can be ready to sell to these potential customers by having translation options available on your home page.

Your programmer can help you set up language choice options for foreign users. Your French isn't what it used to be? Relax—several translation services can reliably translate basic business phrases into major trading languages. AltaVista's Translations Web page, for example, supports German, Italian, French, Spanish, and Portuguese translations from English. Visit it at www.babelfish.altavista.digital.com. You can find many similar services for languages not listed above by keying in the name of a given language as a search term.

International commerce, alas, is not as simple as taking an e-mail order along with the person's Visa number, then shipping to an international address. You will want to educate yourself about taxes, duties, and customs in your target foreign countries, currency conversion, reliable shipping channels, insurance, and what to do in the case of nonpayment or customer dissatisfaction. One place to start your research on the business practices of a specific country is its embassy. See Appendix B for a complete list of embassy e-mail addresses not only for U.S. embassies abroad but also for foreign embassies in the United States.

9 **Give something away.** If this strategy strikes you as counterproductive from a business perspective, your instincts are correct. A grocery store that simply opened its door for a day of free giveaways from the shelves would not necessarily build a loyal customer base—although traffic would be stellar for a day! The art in giving something away is in your wise choice of the recipient. At Graphic Maps, for example, free maps were provided to nonprofit organizations. Their members appreciated this gift and many, in turn, gave Graphic Maps their business.

Contests and prizes serve a similar attention-getting, excitement-building function. The idea that a drawing for $1,000 will be held from among new members on a site's guest book may be just the prod needed to turn some Internet surfers into visitors and customers. If you do develop a contest, be sure that you do not run afoul of the many state and federal laws governing such activities. Needless to say, the "big prize" approach to marketing has been thoroughly abused over the years by merchants who never award a prize at all or those who give merchandise with inflated value and strings attached in lieu of actual prizes. You can steer clear of bad precedent by visiting the Arent Fox Contests and Sweepstakes Internet site (www.arentfox.com), where legal guidelines for such events are clearly explained.

10 **Brand your dot-com everywhere you can. In the case of online businesses, perception is reality.** You have no skyscraper bearing your company name, but neither do the vast majority of the most popular Web sites. If people in your city or region begin to recognize your dot-com name, you're on your way to marketing success. We all find it easier to try the known and familiar rather than the new and untested. We feel somehow safer, and less susceptible to the ridicule of others, when we go with a household name instead of risking business with a newcomer. By placing your dot-com wherever it reasonably might do you some good, you are taking a step to becoming such a recognizable name.

Likely places for your dot-com include every page of printed materials, letterhead, envelopes, business cards, order forms, shipping labels, and other hard-copy stock your business uses; every Internet page pertaining to your business, as well as every e-mail you send and every page of a newsletter you publish; your products, perhaps next to the "Made in (USA, China, etc.)" designation; your business vehicles, checks and deposit slips, license plates; and of course on your place of business, if you are located in a commercial rather than residential area. Other options for publicizing your dot-com name include customer giveaways, such as pens, cups, T-shirts, and so forth. Sponsoring local sports teams or charitable occasions or other high-visibility events can also offer opportunities for placing your dot-com advantageously before the public eye.

News stories about your dot-com can also be extremely valuable for your publicity campaign. Often, the human-interest angle of how you started your own e-business, including the problems you encountered, can appeal to a business journalist for a local newspaper. A friend may be able to plant the seed in the journalist's mind, whereas a direct contact from you might come across as self-serving. You may also want to write a short article about your dot-com experience for one of the hundreds of company, association, and trade magazines listed in *Writer's Market 2000*. Even if you haven't published before, you may have excellent luck placing your story with one or more of these magazines. Unlike *Fortune* and *BusinessWeek*, the trade magazines listed in *Writer's Market 2000* do not have access to a stable of professional writers for their material. Editors of trade magazines are as eager to review your material as you are to get it published.

Thinking outside the Box

EVEN IN THE MIDST OF YOUR MARKETING EFFORTS, REMAIN open to the possibility that an entirely new business paradigm may be what you need to achieve your business goals. For example, one fine-art dealer in New York City spent a small fortune designing a classy Web site, complete with a virtual tour of his galleries, only to experience what so many e-business hopefuls have encountered: no business. Instead of pouring good money after bad to make his original business idea succeed, he stopped in midcourse and tried to "think fresh." He had good product, good pricing, and great service. Therefore, he focused on his one remaining need: increased customer traffic.

In contrast to the one or two hits he was lucky to receive each day at his classy site, the dealer noticed that fine art similar to his offerings was getting hundreds of views per day on auction sites at eBay and Yahoo!. "The next step was obvious," he says, "but hard to take. I folded my previous, expensive Web site and simply listed each of my works on these auction sites. Both eBay and Yahoo! allow me to set a reserve price below which I don't have to sell a particular work. The auction fees are minimal—a few dollars if the auction doesn't produce a sale, and less than 5 percent of the sales price if a sale does result. My overhead in maintaining my own Web site was much greater than those numbers—and I wasn't getting traffic. Now I have about 140 works of fine art listed at auction on any given day. I have more than achieved my financial targets and will stick with the auction approach to business until I can find a way to bring that kind of customer volume directly to my own Web door."

Keeping Your Chin up

THE OLD WISDOM IN SALES AND MARKETING OF ANY KIND GOES as follows: "When you're desperate to sell, no one wants to buy from you; when you're a huge success, everyone wants to buy from you."

The difference between these two conditions lies in your air of confidence. If you're losing and show it, customers shy away. Why do business with someone who seems down-and-out? Pity is not a motivating force for most customers. If you exude optimism and confidence, however, people are eager to join your team, whether as customers, employees, or business partners. The daily mantra for every e-business owner seeking online success should be something along these lines: "Others will follow where I lead. My example creates my future." In short, if you can't be enthusiastic about your e-business efforts, you can't expect others to be. Successful marketing begins inside your head and heart.

Summing Up Step 8

MARKETING AND ADVERTISING AN E-BUSINESS IS MORE COMplicated (and certainly more fun) than putting on similar campaigns for an Old Economy business. As this chapter points out, you have many marketing routes and strategies available to you for promoting your e-business. Best of all, you can usually pursue many of these options at the same time. The key to success lies in exploring and experimenting with the combination of marketing options available to you until you have found the mix best suited to your e-business, your marketplace, and your budget.

9

STEP 9

Find a Trading Community to Support Your E-Business

"NO MAN IS AN ISLAND," wrote John Donne more than three centuries ago. He just as well could have been speaking of Web sites. Like scattered bits of matter after the Big Bang explosion of Internet interest, these points of business light are now moving toward one another and forming recognizable galaxies or, dropping the metaphor for another, e-business communities.

You have probably noticed that your Internet service provider (ISP) or favorite search engine has a "community of merchants" listed on its home page. Since thousands of small companies have signed up to belong to each of these communities, the e-businesses are listed not by name but by category. On the AOL home page, for example, you can click on "Personal Finance" to be connected to advertising for several brokers; on "Travel" to find a dozen or more travel agencies; on "Entertainment" to find music merchants and others; and so forth. The e-business companies involved in this relationship are probably not unlike you: they have evaluated what it would take to guide sufficient traffic to their sites by their own means and have opted instead to get under the big tent of an ISP, albeit at a price, to share in their traffic.

A highly recognizable name—reebok.com, for example—may find it less necessary to buy these "community" services. For most small businesses, however, economies of scope and scale are created when they can attach themselves to an already proven source of steady Internet traffic. The decision for the e-business is not unlike locating in a mall rather than alone on a street corner. Even though the rent tends to be higher in the mall, the additional traffic and resulting business justifies the additional expense.

What the Landlord Does

IN SOME INTERNET MALLS, SUCH AS AMAZON'S ZSHOPS, THE landlord (Amazon in this case) agrees to handle customer service for thousand of items it did not make or distribute. Further, Amazon agrees on behalf of its merchants to guarantee refunds of up to $1,000 for dissatisfied customers. Best of all for the member merchants, Amazon agrees to pay the merchant in full when a buyer fails to pay for a transaction. Not bad! But for these services, Amazon keeps about 15 percent of all gross revenues generated by its family of shops.

Spend a few hours visiting malls within each of the major ISPs and some search engine companies. (If you can't find a mall within this amount of time, there's a good chance no one else can, either.) Visit shops and other forms of e-business in various categories of products and services. Notice how some are highlighted immediately by the host (you can bet they are paying more for this positioning), while others appear in alphabetical or other order. From this sort of research you will be able to locate a few malls where your business might find a happy home. Don't make the mistake of locating only in a mall that has no service similar to yours. A collection of similar services has probably attracted customers' attention to a particular mall in a way that a lone shop or business hasn't.

Once you've narrowed your list of malls to "possibles," contact their marketing directors for a specific description of the terms, conditions, and fees involved in becoming part of the malls. In most cases you will discover that the landlord wants an enrollment (or "subscription") fee in addition to a percentage of overall business.

Business-to-Business Communities

IF YOUR E-BUSINESS WILL BE TRADING PRIMARILY WITH other businesses rather than consumers, you will definitely want to investigate many of the business-to-business (B2B) enclaves rising up in most major industries at present. Here are some of the more stunning success stories of this new way of organizing e-business.

- **Chemdex,** since only late 1998, has positioned itself as an "infomediary" uniting buyers and sellers in the chemical industry into a single, efficient virtual marketplace. Small companies that had little chance of winning contracts with huge firms now use a common online bidding process and can compete in the big leagues. For their part, huge companies that had trouble attracting advantageous bids from small firms are now getting better deals. Chemdex itself makes money by taking a commission on all transactions that take place between members.
- **MetalSiteLP** is a similar B2B community for steel producers and users. It is a joint venture of three competing steel companies—LTV Steel, Steel Dynamics, and Wirton Steel Corp. These firms have pooled their resources to support MetalSite, which makes a market in surplus steel and production overruns. By the end of 2000, MetalSite targeted sales of $30 million per month.
- **Neoforma** (mentioned in Step 3) has created a similar market for health care equipment buyers and sellers over the Internet.

Charlie Finnie, Internet commerce analyst for the San Francisco brokerage firm Volpe Brown Whelan, sees a strong need for such cooperative enclaves. "Industries like steel, paper, and chemicals have not changed the way they do business in more than fifty years, and they need to become more efficient. These infomediaries will help them do that." In the area of chemical production and sales, that efficiency is already apparent, says Finnie: "The reason these companies will be successful is that they will help reduce the cost of doing business." He cites the example of the $100 billion chemical industry, which spends almost $20 billion every year in marketing. "By lowering the cost of sales, you can make chemicals cheaper and help beat competition."

B2B UNDER THE RADAR

WHILE BUSINESS-TO-CONSUMER (B2C) COMPANIES WERE receiving the lion's share of press coverage ("Are you buying holiday gifts on the Internet this year?"), B2B companies were quietly striking understandings and relationships that spelled huge dollars. The Forrester Research Group calculates that in 1998 B2B commerce over the Internet represented $43 billion worth of goods—more than five times the B2C total. By 2002, Forrester has predicted, nearly 10 percent of all B2B transactions would be happening over the Internet—that's 10 percent of $1.3 trillion. Analysts at U.S. Bancorp Piper Jaffray have estimated that by 2001, 90 percent of all e-business transactions would be business-to-business. As *Forbes* pointed out in a February 2000 article, "It also benefits the seller. Say you are a tire manufacturer and you are overstocked on summer tires. Before the Net, you would go to your existing network of buyers, who, knowing you are in a bind, would lowball you. But with global reach, you could peddle your tires to companies in countries with our weather patterns."

The best proof of the pudding of B2B business is General Electric's stunning Web site (geis.com or ge.com/industry) and the business revolution it reveals. In early 2000 GE suffered major breakdowns in its lighting factory in Cleveland. It needed replacement parts fast. Ordinarily, GE would have gone to its standard four suppliers for bids. But with the advent of its new Web site in 2000, GE was able to post its specifications for replacement products on the Internet. The request for quotes drew seven bids, and a Hungarian company won the contract. GE got its parts faster and saved 20 percent in the transaction compared to previous contractors' prices.

The difficulty of opening a Web site such as GE's to the world is a bit of a chicken-and-egg problem. Bidders don't want to go to the effort of signing up until they are sure significant business is at stake. On the other hand, GE doesn't want to commit major contracts to the Internet unless it knows that sufficient qualified bidders are "out there" to accept the work. With the sign-on of such giants as Textron, the GE Web site is in business and already going strong. The Boston-based Yankee Group has asserted that by the end of 2000, $50 billion of the projected $134 billion total B2B commerce over the Internet was expected to have flowed through GE's Web site.

Compare that $50 billion for GE alone to $10 billion, the rosiest estimate for B2C Internet commerce in 2000. Any small business that does not consider becoming linked in a B2B network may be missing the real opportunity of Internet commerce.

An Example of B2B E-Business up Close

BECAUSE BUSINESS-TO-BUSINESS ENCLAVES OF LIKE-MINDED companies are still new, it's appropriate to examine one of these networks in detail. You will then be better informed when choosing a B2B network you may want to join. Selected for review here is the Lightning Manufacturing Project as our in-depth case because it includes so many interesting players: the state of Pennsylvania, the Ingersoll-Rand Company, IBM, and many others. Here is a bold design that has already gone past the experiment stage to begin remodeling (and in part saving) the manufacturing landscape in Pennsylvania and other surrounding states.

The Lightning Manufacturing Project was unveiled by Pennsylvania governor Tom Ridge in October 1999, joined by Ingersoll-Rand CEO Herbert L. Henkel. The Project gathers forty-five small to medium-sized powdered metals producers on one high-powered Web site (lightningmanufacturing.com) where they can learn about the needs of major industrial players—and bid directly and privately to meet those needs.

As a founding partner of the Project, Ingersoll-Rand initially put more than 100 parts, valued at more than $300 million, on the electronic table for machining, forging, or casting by member companies. Lockheed Martin Corp., AlliedSignal Inc., G5 Technologies, Agile Web, Pennsylvania State University, Carnegie Mellon, and Lehigh University are also bringing business and expertise to the Project.

THE BIRTH OF A NOTION

THE LIGHTNING MANUFACTURING PROJECT DEVELOPED AS quickly as its name suggests. A consortium made up of Ingersoll-Rand, IBM, Lockheed Martin, and Cadence Design Systems began negotiations with the Commonwealth of Pennsylvania in May 1999. Governor Ridge agreed to invest $2 million on behalf of the state to help underwrite the development and testing of the system.

In simplest terms, the Project is not unlike a sophisticated online chat room—or, better, an online workshop. A big company says, "Here's what we need." A small company says, "Well, here's what we can deliver." Another party breaks in: "We have advanced technology you should consider. Here's our bid."

The big company couldn't be more pleased to have options to choose from—capitalism doing what it does best. The small companies are delighted to be in the running for contracts they may otherwise have known nothing about. Sooner rather than later, the deal is struck as fast as electrons can whiz confirmations back and forth. The governor of Pennsylvania props his feet on his desk and watches jobs flourish, tax revenues increase, and the Pennsylvania business climate turn toasty. Not a bad return on his $2 million seed money. The envy of neighboring governors is just a dividend.

A NEW BUSINESS MODEL FOR A NEW AGE

THE SYSTEM IS AS COMPLEX AND ADAPTABLE AS THE MODERN business environment requires. At its heart is a new, high-tech business model called the Virtual Corporation Management System. This intellectual engine allows companies to access information, partner or merge with others (often on a temporary or "virtual" basis), and do business literally at the speed of light.

"The Lightning Manufacturing Project has the potential to revolutionize the speed with which companies can collaborate and deliver products," says Governor Ridge. "This project, with the Virtual Corporation Management System (VCMS) at its core, will allow manufacturing industries across the commonwealth to compete and flourish in the digital economy of the future."

LIGHTNING AIMED AT BUSINESS PROBLEMS

AMERICAN INDUSTRIES OF ALL SIZES HAVE LONG PRESSED their noses to the window of the Asian arrangement whereby government works actively to promote the welfare and profitability of both state and private companies. In the United States industry relations with government at all levels have more often been a tug-of-war of opposed interests. Companies try to pull their weight in the form of jobs and taxes, and government usually pulls back with time-consuming, expensive regulatory processes and a plethora of initiative-killing forms, codes, and procedures.

The Lightning Manufacturing Project, by contrast, aims at what Governor Ridge calls "friction-free government." In fact, his state inaugurated a flagship Web site, www.paopen4business, to promote what the governor calls "an overhaul of outmoded corporate and business regulations that impede the creation of virtual enterprises and networks."

WHERE THE PEDAL MEETS THE METAL

HERE'S A SPECIFIC EXAMPLE OF HOW THE LIGHTNING MANUfacturing Project has worked in its initial rollout. (The business model and technology are undergoing constant scrutiny and refinement as new industries come aboard.) Small to medium-sized Pennsylvania powdered metals companies had long had the problem of diminished economies of scale when it comes to finding out about available work, preparing detailed responses to industry requests for proposal (RFPs), and building credibility with industrial giants. At the same time, companies such as Ingersoll-Rand had their own set of problems seeking out the right manufacturer for the right job—preferably right away, certifying quality standards and costs in advance, and knitting together the often elaborate business and legal threads of new business dealings.

Add to these nail-biters the government and citizens of Pennsylvania, who depend on the success of both large and small companies for jobs and taxes. At stake is the welfare of participating Pennsylvania companies that employ 20,000 workers and purchase more than $700 million worth of Pennsylvania-made products each year. North-central Pennsylvania is home to sixty powdered metals producers, representing nearly 70 percent of the $4.5 billion industry. Employment in recent years has stagnated.

In the past, traditional state government efforts to support companies by tax breaks and job training haven't meant much when no business is coming in the door. As one business owner put it, "Taxing me less when I'm earning nothing is like giving a free haircut to a bald man."

The problems of all three parties were targeted by a bolt from the blue suits leading the Lightning Manufacturing Project. Using the VCMS Web-based architecture, small to medium companies can learn directly from industrial giants such as Ingersoll-Rand what needs doing, when, and where. Ingersoll-Rand can put parts projects out for bid to dozens of competing companies, all linked electronically not only to sources of information crucial to the bidding process but also to proposal-creation tools, fast ways to certify quality compliance and business know-how and history, and joint-venturing connections for companies that don't want to go it alone. Ingersoll-Rand expects to save 25 percent in fabrication costs, while Pennsylvania powdered metals companies estimate that the Project will increase purchases of Pennsylvania industrial products by 10 percent per year.

PROTECTING THE PROPRIETARY INTERESTS OF MEMBERS

FIRE WALLS WITHIN THE PROJECT SYSTEM PREVENT THE LEAKage of business secrets from one company to the next. Especially in the case of small businesses, a handful of proprietary techniques spell competitive advantage. Once spilled, those secrets flow immediately to the competition and often seal the fate of the company that lost them.

As noted previously, the Lightning Manufacturing Project initially focused primarily on the powdered metals and industrial electronics sectors in Pennsylvania. Within a year of rollout, however, the Project's scope widened to include more of the fourteen additional industries targeted for inclusion. The ultimate goal of the Lightning Manufacturing Project, according to Jim Bacchus, Ingersoll-Rand's director of business processes and strategic technologies, "is to take the chaos out of doing business on the Internet." By building into the system reliable standards and ways to certify products and services, time-consuming prepurchase investigations and associated costly errors can be eliminated. A code of ethics also can be nurtured and enforced among Project members, says Bacchus, so that collaborating companies "can develop trust at the speed of light."

Step through the Project's first doorway, the World Wide Powdered Metallurgy Commerce Portal, along with the general business public, as they did in the first quarter of 2000. As they enter, small manufacturers can't help but glimpse dollar signs through this portal; Ingersoll-Rand planned to use this system to spend much of the $20 million the company earmarked in 2000 for powdered metal parts. Other partner companies including Lockheed Martin also have attractive purchasing targets.

The time- and money-saving marvels available down this electronic rabbit hole would amaze even Alice. Here customers can:

- post requests for quotes (RFQs);
- select suppliers to whom they want their information to flow;
- provide these suppliers with drawings, technical specifications, and other details necessary for accurate bidding; and
- advise the supplier of due dates, terms, conditions, and other contractual requirements.

Suppliers, on the other hand, can use the same system to receive notification of bidding opportunities, access all pertinent information, make easy use of a standardized bidding template, and post questions back to the customer seeking the bid. As a case in point, Ingersoll-Rand has more than 2 million drawings available online through the Powdered Metallurgy Commerce Portal. Suppliers can review this wealth of information in close detail during the bid preparation process. Through direct electronic communication links, the customer and supplier can quickly work through the inevitable questions, clarifications, and change requests that accompany a technical manufacturing project. Because all suppliers use the same bidding template, the customer can compare "apples to apples" in selecting the right supplier.

The customer avoids the phenomenon of "bid blizzard" (too many bids to process efficiently) by completing a registration process that determines supplier qualifications. The customer can decide whether to post a bid only for qualified suppliers or open the procurement cycle to any supplier. Proprietary information given by suppliers is protected so that competitors don't peek or poach.

A virtual bar without drinks (well, without stools or peanuts, either) is provided where both suppliers and customers can kick around ideas, questions, problems, and possibilities. The Discussion Topics center within the Powdered Metallurgy Commerce Portal allows any registered user to create or join an online discussion among member suppliers, customers, industry experts, and university pooh-bahs. Users can search the entire discussion database for the latest technology directions, breakthroughs, and insights in the powdered metallurgy industry. Resource Links allow users to click through to industry facts, directories and guides, conferences, associations, industry standards, publications, and employment opportunities. Finally, the Ask the Professor link connects the user via e-mail to faculty experts at Pennsylvania State University for help with specific technical issues.

AND BEHIND DOOR TWO...

THE ELECTRONICS INFUSION PORTAL ATTRACTS CUSTOMERS and suppliers by its promise of faster new-product development using the collaborative capabilities in advanced electronics of its Certified Business Network members. Assembling the right team of people or companies for an electronics development project can now be a matter of minutes or hours rather than weeks or months. The resulting "virtual corporation" may exist just for the duration of the project, with all participants then returning to their former situations. Or the fledgling group may grow into a more long-term contractor for similar projects in the future.

As might be expected, the Electronics Infusion Portal shares many of the features of the Powdered Metallurgy Commerce Portal, but with several happy wrinkles of its own. The Subscription page lets users select a variety of ways to be notified about project developments and activity—by project title, author, or object type, or by particular documents. When users create their subscription, they can opt to be notified by e-mail, digital pager, or even digital phone. Enhancements just around the corner at the Electronics Infusion Portal include easy calendar and database integration to personal data accessing devices such as the PalmPilot and to groupware, including Lotus Notes.

WHEN A DOOR ISN'T

THE BRAINCHILDREN OF THE FUTURE USUALLY HAVE TO WEAR the hand-me-down language of another era. For example, metaphors such as "door" and "portal" suggest a relatively fixed conceptual architecture where passages lead to places. But entering a portal of the Lightning Manufacturing Project is less like walking into a building than it is like swimming in deep water. Freed from external structures and barriers, you can dive or float without constraint. As Mark Lang, executive director of Ben Franklin Technology Partners, points out, the genius of the virtual enterprise encouraged by Lightning Manufacturing lies precisely in such freedom. This new way of business "is constantly recreating itself—forming to meet a need, dissolving when the need is satisfied, and then reconfiguring with different players, resources, and skill sets when the next need comes along. There are no rigid hierarchies that determine how it responds to the marketplace. That means that untapped capacity is put to revenue-producing use instead of draining a company's resources."

The "backroom plumbing" that makes the Lightning Manufacturing Project work is the same type of process that works for GE and Chemdex: a robust software system all members can easily access. Bidding procedures are simplified. The back-and-forth of questions about materials and specifications is handled by e-mails instead of reports. Supportive relationships grow among member companies as they enjoy smooth transactions with one another.

Because e-business protocols are standardized for all members of a trading network like Chemdex, you will want to design your e-business site in close coordination with other members' templates and examples, and probably with considerable use of the same software others use. Check with the administrator of any trading network you wish to join to learn how to set up your Web site for uniformity and compatibility with other members.

Summing Up Step 9

BUSINESS-TO-BUSINESS E-COMMERCE HAS, IN GENERAL, BEEN significantly more successful than business-to-consumer sites, whether mom-and-pop operations or e-spin-offs from major retailers such as Sears and WalMart. Becoming part of such a trading community involves at least four components: (1) having something valuable to offer the community of participating companies; (2) being willing to adapt your e-business operation to protocols, codes, and procedures already in place for the trading community; (3) doing business efficiently and reputably, so as not to damage your business image in the trading community; and (4) moving forward at all times with operational improvements and marketing initiatives that consolidate your role as a player among the participating companies.

1

STEP 10

Build Your E-Business Team

THIS STEP AND THE NEXT BITE OFF A HUGE piece of business strategy and practice: the human side of running an e-business. Instead of tripping lightly through a myriad of management topics, let's focus on the twelve management areas that matter the most for e-business success:

1. How to spot management pitfalls and avoid disaster
2. How to hire effectively and legally in a tight job market
3. How to meld a diversity of talents into a single team
4. How to get competitive salary information for a number of job categories, based on your region
5. How to find, evaluate, and hire a consultant, if one is needed
6. When to consider increasing your staff
7. What to consider when hiring an attorney or accountant for your e-business needs
8. How to handle the issue of stock options or other compensation beyond the salary

9 How to position your company for later sale

Step 11, "Manage Your E-Business Team," covers the rest:

10 How to motivate yourself and your employees

11 How to run a tight ship in terms of employee integrity

12 How to manage knowledge and change in your e-business

Doing these twelve things well will provide the kind of day-to-day stability in your e-business that you will need if you want to find time to explore other skills and strategies as an e-business manager.

Consumer Management Pitfalls

WHEN YOU'RE IN THE FAST LANE OF ENTHUSIASM ON the way to starting your own e-business, it's easy to ignore obstacles in your path—until it's too late. This portion of Step 10 reminds you of eight potholes that can spell disaster for any new e-venture.

1. 'I Didn't Know Management Would Take So Much Time.'

ESPECIALLY IF YOU ARE MAKING THE TRANSITION FROM employment with a larger company or institution, many time-consuming management functions may have been almost invisible to you. Someone else took care of office supplies, retirement contributions, regulatory filings, health plans, payroll, accounting, performance reviews, basic site maintenance, business planning, IT management, and all the other details of business life. Now many of these nettlesome matters land on your desk, even after you have delegated them. The point: Plan liberally for management time as part of your new schedule.

2. 'I Thought I Had Enough Money.'

IT'S ALMOST A CLICHÉ—UNFORTUNATELY, A TRUE CLICHÉ—that many new e-ventures fail due to undercapitalization. You've no doubt computed how many customers you'll require to break even and, over time, to show a profit. But have you also computed the time it may take to achieve such patronage? The point: Be realistic about how long you can sustain your business as it builds a clientele.

3. 'A New Competitor Stole My Clients.'

YOUR MARKETING AND DEMOGRAPHIC SURVEYS FOR YOUR e-business probably looked rosy before you took the plunge into your company. But those surveys may not have taken into account the second-wave phenomenon. The concept isn't subtle: an unseen competitor waits for you—the first wave—to spend your money and energies creating a clientele in your region of cyberspace, then comes in as the second wave to underprice you and reap the benefits of your start-up work. The point: Work out strategies in advance to cope with potential competition.

4. 'They Quit Just When I Needed Them the Most!'

IF THE SUCCESS OF YOUR NEW VENTURE DEPENDS DIRECTLY on your employees Fred, Linda, and Juan continuing to perform their specialties, you should play through a business scenario in which any or all of them resign. Can you rehire for those specialties in your area? Can you keep your site open for business while you're seeking replacements for key employees? The point: Build an e-business plan that makes provisions for unexpected transitions in key employee categories.

5. 'I Lost My Lease.'

CONTRARY TO POPULAR MYTH, E-BUSINESSES DO END UP WITH a certain commitment to bricks-and-mortar business space. With commercial rents rising dramatically in many regions of the country, many landlords won't lock in to long lease terms. Instead, they may offer an attractive short-term rate that gets you to sign on the bottom line but makes no promises for the long term. Perhaps you assume that by being a good tenant you will be able to renew your lease in the future at a rate not much higher than your starting rate. Or you may assume that your upcoming success will more than accommodate any reasonable rent increase. Wrong. Once your e-business shows its profitability, your landlord may well decide to double or triple your rent when your lease comes up for renewal. Your complaints about rent-gouging won't mean much to a landlord who has a new tenant willing to take the property at the higher rate. The point: Base your financial planning as much as possible on certainties, not assumptions.

6. 'I Thought I Was Protected.'

EVEN FRIVOLOUS AND UNFOUNDED LAWSUITS MAY TAKE YEARS and thousands of dollars in legal fees to put aside. In the meantime, your ability to acquire additional business financing may be compromised. Why? Because you have to answer "yes" to the business loan application question "Are you a party to a lawsuit?" A disgruntled customer or vendor may never get a dime from you when the dust of legal wrangles has settled—but his or her suit for hundreds of thousands of dollars is nonetheless a matter of public record until it is resolved. The point: Plan not only for adequate insurance but also for legal defense funding and strategies that will prevent legal troubles from spilling over into financial troubles for your e-business.

7. 'I Didn't Plan On Getting Sick.'

IT'S AN UNWELCOME THOUGHT, BUT A NECESSARY ONE: WHAT happens to your venture if you must take time off because of illness or other circumstances? Owner/operator incapacity ranks second only to undercapitalization as the cause of e-business failure. The success of your venture should not depend exclusively on your ability to keep up the pace without missing a beat. The point: Develop backup plans that can see your professional venture through difficult personal times.

8. 'I Couldn't Stop Celebrating.'

ADMITTEDLY, THERE IS UNDERSTANDABLE EXCITEMENT AND euphoria associated with starting an e-business of your own. In the weeks prior to opening your site, you seem to be writing large checks to everyone. Nothing is too good for the office—expensive carpet, chic furniture, impressive artwork, the more the better. Or your penchant may be office equipment ("the most powerful new computers"), prominence in community affairs ("we sponsor six youth teams"), or advertising ("banner ads everywhere"). As helpful as any one of these can be to business success, they can quickly become too much of a good thing. The point: Stick to a business model that values profitability over ego gratification.

STEERING SAFELY AROUND THESE EIGHT POTHOLES OF NEW-business failure can keep your e-venture moving forward as you intended.

Recruiting and Hiring the Right People—in the Right Way

YOU CERTAINLY REMEMBER THE DAYS WHEN YOU DOUBTED whether you could ever afford to hire help. But here you are: even in a tight job market, you've had reasonably good response to your "career opportunity" notices placed on job sites such as www.monster.com and www.careertrack.com as well as in area newspapers. Some of your best recruiting luck has come as a result of calling placement directors at colleges and universities in your region. You had a chance to contact lots of fresh talent before they were lured to bigger firms.

You've now lined up interviews for eight of your top contenders for two available positions. You're excited at the prospect of bringing new talent into your e-business. You want the interview process to help you determine who's right for the job.

Because e-businesses typically exist on a fast track, owners and managers may tend to interview and hire "by the seat of the pants"—that is, without a rational interview system or adequate means of comparison among job candidates. The result, too often, is that the flash in the pan that seemed so promising in the slapdash interview proves to be a disaster and liability on the job. Even worse, such unreflective hiring practices can land an e-business in court for illegal employment practices under Equal Employment Opportunity Commission (EEOC) guidelines and other legislation.

To hire well, e-business owners and managers will do well to understand and practice a relatively new interview strategy now used by the majority of *Fortune* 500 companies and most government agencies. Called behavior-based structured interviewing (BSI), this method ensures that candidates will receive equal treatment in the interview process, that interview questions will relate to job responsibilities, and that those candidates who can perform job-related tasks will score highest in the interview process. In other words, BSI helps e-businesses choose winners.

WHAT'S WRONG WITH OLD-STYLE INTERVIEWING?

"OUR INTERVIEWERS LIKE THE SEAT-OF-THE-PANTS APPROACH to hiring," one Texas e-auction administrator told me. "It makes the interview more lively. You never know what you'll end up discussing with an applicant." She pointed out that experienced interviewers like to trust their intuition—their gut feelings—to come up with the right questions and pick the right candidate.

This set of ideas is the general defense for old-fashioned

interviewing. In addition to the arguments this manager made, old-style interviewing has the weight of history on its side—it's "the way we've always done it"—and, in fact, it's the way most of us were interviewed for our present jobs.

But put yourself in the place of a job applicant for, let's say, systems analyst. You are one among several candidates to be interviewed. Does it matter that the big boss in the office interviewed your competition, but you are to be interviewed by a lower-ranking manager? That the previous interviewee was taken out to lunch and you're "next up" at 2 P.M. in a cramped office meeting room? Of course it does. In traditional interviewing, the judgments of individual interviewers (and their relative clout in the company) can vary widely. If you're lucky, you will get an interviewer who likes you and has the status to help you get the job. The operative word is lucky—the process isn't fair or rational.

Note that in this old-style interview, questions come out of the blue, according to the whim of the interviewer. At worst, these questions are time wasters for both the company and the applicant—just talk that yields little valuable information about the candidate's suitability for the position. Freed from any interview plan, the typical old-style interviewer does up to 80 percent of the talking during the interview.

THE LEGAL BASIS FOR STRUCTURED INTERVIEWING

TO ALL SUCH MATTERS OF CHANCE, GUT FEELINGS, AND potential bias, the law related to hiring says "Stop!" Specifically, the Uniform Guidelines arising out of Title VII and EEOC legislation insist that the interview be designed on the basis of specific job requirements. Both the content and method of the interview must be developed to reveal accurately and fairly which candidates are best qualified to fulfill the job requirements determined by the company. If challenged in court, employers must be able to show that interview questions are directly related to these job requirements. In addition, employers must afford each candidate equal treatment in the screening process.

DEVELOPING THE JOB ANALYSIS AND DESCRIPTION

A JOB ANALYSIS TEAM—PERHAPS ONLY TWO PEOPLE IN A small e-business—is usually composed of a manager deeply familiar with the job and one or more people who are good at the job. The team meets to organize the many critical-incident descriptions into a succinct description of job behaviors—the "job description." The panel also considers the following issues:

- **Information sources of particular importance for the job.** Must the applicant, for example, be thoroughly familiar with a certain set of state or federal regulations? A particular database system?
- **Abilities in decision making or information processing critical to job performance.** Must the applicant be able to perform some mathematical operations in his or her head? Hold several numbers in mind at once? Review numbers or programming code quickly for accuracy?
- **Physical requirements, including coordination, stress, and dexterity.** Must the applicant be able to sustain periods of prolonged work stress during crunch times in the office? Sit at the computer or other office machines for hours at a time without physical problems?
- **Social skills required for the job.** Will the job entail the tactful supervision of others? Meeting clients in high-stakes, stressful contexts? Relating to coworkers as a motivational manager?
- **Scheduling and travel requirements of the job.** Must the applicant be ready to make scheduling changes and travel plans on short notice? Is the candidate available for overtime?

These types of items form the complete job description, only a summary of which will probably appear in newspaper or online help-wanted ads for the position. "But all this might take a few hours!" comes the predictable complaint. Right—and those few hours are a wise investment of time when compared to the months and years, perhaps, that the company may have to suffer with the wrong hire, all due to inadequate, ill-considered job descriptions or interviewing techniques.

To keep your interview process fair and objective, all questions developed for a structured interview are based on the job description and should be asked in the same order for each applicant.

DOCUMENTING THE STRUCTURED INTERVIEW

MANAGERS AND OWNERS IN E-BUSINESSES HAVE GOOD REASON to protect themselves against potential charges of discrimination in hiring. Most plaintiffs to date are successful in such suits, and court awards regularly run into the hundreds of thousands of dollars, especially when legal fees are included.

If a hiring discrimination suit is brought against your company, the court will insist on knowing the following information. These items are must-haves for documentation of the interview process:

1 **Document the job analysis process.** How is the job defined? How did you determine the specific behaviors necessary for performing the job successfully?

2 **Document the process by which questions were created.** Who participated in their creation? Why were these people deemed competent to create the questions? How does each question asked in the interview relate to a behavior necessary for performing the job? In what ways do the number, type, and arrangement of questions reflect the proportionate importance of particular behaviors necessary to perform the job?

3 **Document the system by which applicant responses were evaluated.** What is the system? Who created standards for the evaluation of responses? How do these benchmark responses relate to real levels of success among those actually performing the job? Were raw scores handled statistically? What weighting, if any, was used in the analysis of scores?

4 **Document the process of interviewing candidates.** How did applicants find out about the job? What were the criteria for choosing those applicants who were invited for interviews? Where and when were interviews conducted? Who served as interviewers? What are their qualifications, especially in relation to the job at hand? How were questions delivered? How were responses noted? How long did interviews last? How did different interviews compare in

time, content of questions, and method of evaluation?

5. **Document applicant responses and scores.** Notes taken by interviewers must be easily interpretable in reconstructing the approximate content of an applicant's response.
6. **Document the specific process by which one applicant was chosen over the others.** What factors were involved? What was the weighting of those factors?
7. **Document the validity of the interview process.** Does the process in fact predict job performance?

Certainly the work involved in conducting effective, legal interviews compares favorably, when facing a lawsuit, to the more dangerous course of trying to construct or fabricate a legally defensible hiring procedure after the fact. And why do disappointed job applicants sue? You name it: allegations of age discrimination, ethnic bias, gender preference, violations of the Americans with Disabilities Act (see Appendix C), and so forth. A small e-business is no less vulnerable than an e-business giant as the target of such suits.

EXAMPLES OF USEFUL BEHAVIOR-BASED INTERVIEW QUESTIONS

WHAT AN APPLICANT HAS DONE IS A BETTER INDICATOR OF future job success than what the applicant believes, feels, thinks, or knows. The following questions are useful in getting applicants to discuss work realities rather than notions or suppositions.

- Tell me how you increased teamwork among a previous group with whom you worked.
- Describe what you liked and disliked about how you were managed in previous positions.
- Recall a time when you made what you consider a mistake or a bad decision on the job. How did you handle the situation?
- In your past work life, what kind of coworkers or clients rubbed you the wrong way? How did you respond?
- Tell me about a time when you set specific work goals for yourself. How did things turn out?
- Describe a time when you had to criticize or discipline the performance of someone who worked with you or for you. How did you handle the situation? What was the result?

- Walk me through the major highlights of your career so far and tell me where you want to go next.
- Tell me about a work emergency or crisis of some kind in which you were involved. What was your role? What did you do?
- We've all felt stress in our work lives. Tell me about work-related situations that cause stress for you. How do you typically handle such stress?
- In your most recent position, what did you learn? How did you apply this learning?
- Tell me about a challenge you faced in a previous work situation. How did you respond?
- Every manager has to learn to delegate well. Describe a work situation in which you delegated responsibility successfully. Then tell me about a time when your delegation of responsibility did not work out well. How did you handle that situation?
- What approaches worked best for you in the past in communicating with your boss? With your coworkers? With your subordinates?
- Tell me about a time when you took charge as a leader in a work situation without being formally assigned to that role by your boss.
- What experiences have you had working with people of different ethnicities, ages, or physical ability levels?
- In the past have you had a preference for working mainly with men or women? Explain your answer.
- Tell me about a time when you felt you went beyond the call of duty in helping a customer.

USEFUL PROBES FOR INTERVIEWING

ALTHOUGH PROBING FOR MORE EXTENSIVE ANSWERS FROM candidates is not considered an appropriate approach in strictly structured interviewing environments, the practice is still widely used. The technique can be applied fairly if each candidate is given approximately the same degree of probing by interviewers.

- Please clarify what you mean by . . .
- How did you feel when that happened?

- Why do you think you reacted as you did?
- Did you consider other options at the time?
- Please give me more details about . . .
- How do you think others felt about your actions at the time?
- Looking back on the experience, how do you see things now?
- What was going through your mind when you took that action?
- Did the outcome of your action satisfy you?

Melding a Diversity of Talents into a Single Team

SO, AFTER SOME LAST-MINUTE NEGOTIATING ON TELECOMmuting privileges and a slight bump in salary, you've got your two new hires. With luck you'll be adding several more later in the year. You already sense that your role as company founder, technical problem solver, public relations source, and chief bottle washer has begun to change. Now you're responsible for wise delegation, role definitions, project assignments, and employee evaluation. In short, you're a manager.

You don't want to be guilty of trying to force square pegs into round holes. In the high-stakes world of e-business, employees who just don't fit can be a drag on company profits, productivity, and day-to-day fun. You've met these individuals—men and women leading professional lives of "quiet desperation," in Thoreau's words. When they change employers, as they do often, they leave in their wake broken projects and sour relationships. The American Management Association estimates that an employer pays about a year's salary in termination costs, selection interviewing, hiring, and training to replace an employee who just didn't work out.

If you were dealing with hardware or software, such compatibility problems would have been obvious from the beginning. But these new human parts of your business network don't come with reliable spec sheets. Only after the fact of hiring do you discover where they will work out best, if at all.

CONSIDER A PERSONALITY TEST

JUST AS WE DIFFER IN HANDEDNESS (RIGHT OR LEFT), SO DO many psychologists propose that we have "personality tendencies" that play out through our entire lives, personal and professional. These tendencies to feel and behave according to our own largely fixed habits of mind can be viewed as a series of four continua:

Extroversion------------/----Introversion
Sensing------------------/-Intuitive
Thinking--/--------------Feeling
Perceiving---------------/-Judging

The person measured in the example above is strong on the Judging scale, lost without his or her Day-timer, Gantt time charts, and meticulous filing system. Add personality tendencies toward Introversion (as opposed to comfort and pleasure in the company of others), Thinking (rational analysis versus perceptive emotion), and Intuitive (big-picture thinking versus detail orientation), and you have the whole personality package of this individual.

So what? That question has been answered—painfully—by more than one e-business manager trying to get employees to work together productively. Let's say one of your new hires is very different in personality type from the individual profiled above. Your new hire's personality type, ENTJ (for dominance in Extroversion, Intuitive, Thinking, and Judging), predictably will conflict with the first personality profile.

Fortune reports an example of such confrontation: shortly after David Carpenter took over as CEO of Transamerica Occidental Life Insurance, he summoned two executives to breathe life into the company's dusty five-year management plan. Carpenter and executive vice president Simon Baitler began speculating about the new "vision" and "picture" they wanted the plan to communicate. The other executive sat silent, as if confused. "He just didn't get it," Baitler says. "We're talking pictures, but he's looking for details. To him, we're not even talking the English language."

A TEST FOR UNDERSTANDING OUR PERSONALITY TENDENCIES

JUST AFTER WORLD WAR II THE MOTHER-DAUGHTER TEAM OF Katherine Briggs and Isabel Briggs Myers developed an easy-to-administer test for determining personality predispositions. Widely known now as the Myers-Briggs Type Inventory (MBTI), marketed by Consulting Psychologists Press in Palo Alto, California, the test poses about 100 questions such as the following:

- Would you rather work for someone who is always kind or always fair?
- In a group, do you often introduce others, or wait to be introduced?
- Do you find it harder to adapt to routine or to more-or-less constant change?

The answers to these sorts of questions, "bubbled in" on a computer answer sheet, lead to a profile of the test taker's personality tendencies. In 1998 more than 3 million people took the MBTI, at an average cost of $10 per test. Companies that have used the test widely across employee levels include GE, Honeywell, AT&T, Lucent Technologies, Citicorp, Apple, Exxon, AlliedSignal, 3M, and others. It turns out that about 60 percent of businessmen are strong on the Thinking dimension, and 60 percent of businesswomen are strong on Feeling. Interestingly, both male and female top executives tend to be INTJ (Introverted, Intuitive, Thinking, and Judging). A disproportionate number of executives with this personality profile rise to become CEOs.

SO WHAT'S A PERSONALITY TEST GOOD FOR?

ALTHOUGH ITS TEST IS BY FAR THE MOST POPULAR ON THE market, Consulting Psychologists Press has stopped short of explicitly recommending the MBTI as the sole standard by which people should be hired (or, for that matter, fired). The validity of the test is not so finely determined as to withstand legal challenge by a job seeker who is turned down simply because of the results of a personality test. But the test can be vastly useful for the following tasks:

- **Self-discovery,** including understanding what you like and dislike about your job.
- **Conflict prevention and resolution.** Once you know your own personality needs and tendencies, you are forearmed to deal strategically instead of blindly with those whose personality types run counter to yours.
- **Team building.** Knowing your coworkers' personality types gives you a leg up on building strong, complementary work teams. Especially in the fast-paced, high-stakes environment of e-business design and management, you would probably not want a work team made up entirely of Judging personalities (great on planning but inflexible to change), Intuitive personalities (awake to the big picture but weak on the details), and so forth. The best of all possible worlds for team building is a group of individuals whose personalities complement but do not clone one another's strengths.

Interested in exploring your personality type and those of your employees, with an eye toward making compatible work assignments and building strong work teams? A brief and widely used version of a Jungian personality test appears in my 1997 book, *Winning with Difficult People* (Barron's). The test is comprised of sixty yes/no questions and takes no more than thirty minutes to complete. A self-scoring guide is attached to the test. By understanding a bit more of what makes the individuals in your organization tick, you can act intelligently and strategically as a manager to nurture talents, including your own.

The Hiring Scene

COMPETITIVE SALARIES

YOUR EMPLOYMENT AD PROBABLY INCLUDES A VAGUE phrase such as "excellent compensation for qualified candidate"—but what does excellent mean in your region? How do you know if you're offering too little to attract high-quality candidates or offering too much? Unfortunately, no Department of Labor publication is current enough or regionally specific enough to help you pin down salary ranges for the various occupations involved in e-business. What's more, the range of salaries can vary widely, depending whether e-business in your area is facing boom or bust times. In California's Silicon Valley, starting salaries for programmers began to plummet in the spring and summer of 2000 as financially strapped dot-coms made massive cuts in their workforce.

The most reliable way to obtain current salary information for your industry and region is to ask job candidates to supply a salary history (many will comply) and, at the same time, to involve yourself in Rotary organizations, industry associations, or other networking groups of businesspeople where information is often shared informally. Local business publications and newspapers can also be good sources of up-to-date salary information if the article writer or reporter has done his or her homework well. If the article at hand seems to be written purely for its sensationalism ("Six Figures for a Lucky College Graduate!"), seek out a print or Internet source that provides statistical information for a wider group.

You can also simply test the market. If the salary range you're offering brings you few candidates and no winners, you obviously will have to bump it up a bit to the threshold of regional comparables. This process, however, has the disadvantage of wasting your time in making your new hire. The time you spend trying to save $10,000 may be ill-considered if it costs your company several times that amount in lost momentum, market share, and sales due to understaffing.

HOW TO FIND, EVALUATE, AND HIRE A CONSULTANT

INSTEAD OF HIRING A PERMANENT EMPLOYEE, YOU MAY WANT to hire a consultant on a daily, weekly, or project basis. Although you will no doubt pay more per hour for this individual than for a permanent employee, you probably won't pay benefits or other add-ons. Depending on the contract you strike with the consultant, you probably also retain the right to end the consultancy if you're not getting the results you want.

Word-of-mouth recommendations can be useful so long as they do not come from your direct competitors, who are unlikely to pass along a hero consultant to help you. In addition, there are consultant providers in most major cities.

These agencies can give you a complete description of the person's expertise, services, and fees. In some cases, the agencies bond the consultant and guarantee confidentiality for any work he or she performs for you. Locate such agencies through the Internet or paper Yellow Pages, using the search words "consultants" or "business consultants." Local colleges and universities often can be good sources of expertise, both from the ranks of the faculty in such fields as computer science and e-commerce and from the graduate student population.

Although many consultants may not be free to describe specific projects for named clients (due to confidentiality agreements), they should nonetheless be willing to give you a thorough summary of the kinds of work they have performed and the general results they have achieved. You can also expect a reputable consultant to have several references you can contact.

In hiring a consultant, it is to your advantage to write down in a contract, however brief, the specific terms of the work, any confidentiality requirements, the time constraints or deadlines, and the agreed-upon fee and schedule for payment. Some consultants ask for a retainer, against which they will bill their initial work. Others agree to invoice you on a regular basis for work performed. For short-term projects, you can probably negotiate a "payment upon completion" arrangement with the consultant. The consultant may well present you with his or her preferred contract. Read it carefully; you have no obligation to use this document, and you may find it advantageous to work up a contract of your own that expresses the business relationship from your perspective.

WHEN DO YOU NEED MORE EMPLOYEES?

THERE IS NO MAGIC FORMULA BASED ON PROFITABILITY, market share, gross revenues, or other measure that will tell you when you should hire more help. If your budget permits, you can gauge your need for more employees by your own workload. If you are sufficiently distracted from your job description that the company or your own well-being is threatened, it's time to find qualified help. You may want to experiment with a temporary employee (from a temp agency, perhaps) to test your staffing needs. You may also try to hire a part-time employee, with the idea of increasing his role to full-time if needed.

WHAT TO CONSIDER WHEN HIRING AN ATTORNEY OR ACCOUNTANT FOR YOUR E-BUSINESS

BOTH THESE INDIVIDUALS WILL BE VITAL CONTRIBUTORS TO your e-business success—if you choose them with care. It is wise to engage both your attorney and your accountant well before you find yourself facing a lawsuit or an IRS audit. These professionals typically charge more when they are brought in at the last minute to pick up the pieces. In addition, they may not be available to you at the eleventh hour unless you've developed a professional relationship with them earlier.

Both attorneys and accountants are used to being interviewed—even grilled—as a precursor to being hired. You should feel comfortable asking the hard questions: "How much experience do you have in e-business law [or accounting]?" "How many e-business clients do you now serve? Can I talk to some of them about your services?" "What can you do for me and my business?" Reaching a firm understanding about fees can be difficult with both attorneys and accountants. Although they may quote you an hourly rate, their total charges are usually left unspecified, "depending on what's involved." You should feel comfortable discussing fees and reviewing work with your chosen attorney or accountant. An individual who makes you feel awkward for bringing up fees probably isn't your best choice.

HOW TO HANDLE THE ISSUE OF STOCK OPTIONS AND OTHER FORMS OF COMPENSATION

AT LAST COUNT, SEVERAL HUNDRED SECRETARIES AND OTHER hourly workers at Microsoft had found themselves millionaires, thanks to a regular trickle of stock options over the years. The well-established practice in e-business of offering stock options to employees and investors as an inducement to a business relationship has proven especially useful for cash-strapped enterprises. Through stock options, investors or employees share the risk with the entrepreneur/founder and enjoy the rewards, if and when they come.

How many stock options, and of what sort, to offer employees or others can't be estimated, even in a general way. Your attorney, CPA, or accountant is the best source for such information. They will consider your e-business legal structure (corporation, partnership, and so on) as well as your tax situation in helping you develop a sound plan for offering options. Most entrepreneurs take special care not to give away so many options that control of the company could be wrested away from the founder.

How to Position Your Company for Later Sale

IT'S NOT UNUSUAL IN THE WORLD OF E-BUSINESS FOR AN EXIT strategy to be included in the original business plan for the enterprise. The founder of the company may decide, for example, to develop the e-business through the IPO (initial public offering) stage, then to sell out his or her interest when control is assumed by a corporate board of directors.

No matter what the timing for sale, four rules apply to preparing the company for transfer of ownership:

1 **Maintain squeaky-clean financial records that have been audited in a scheduled way by a reputable accounting firm.** Efforts to cook the books in a last-minute attempt to make the business more salable are a formula for lawsuits.
2 **Be able to show the relation of the company's progress to your business plan.** Are you ahead of target projections? Behind? If your e-business has evolved significantly so that the original business plan is now outdated, prepare a revised business plan showing the nature of the changes in the company and the projected impact of those changes.
3 **Make sure that key company assets, including knowledge assets, are transferable.** If patents, trademarks, copyright, or other legal protections are part of your e-business assets, seek the advice of your attorney in how to transfer these as part of the sale of the company. If you or other

key employees are agreeing to stay on for a specified period to help run the company or provide transition training for others, make sure the terms of such employment and related compensation are fully spelled out.

4 **Time your sale in an advantageous way.** Most companies cycle through up and down periods. Putting your company up for sale at the wrong time (the "fire sale" mistake) can reduce your profits substantially. A business broker can be a helpful ally in advising you how to advertise your e-business for sale, what price to ask, and what terms to negotiate.

Summing Up Step 10

NO MATTER WHAT THEIR TECHNOLOGICAL COMPLEXITY, e-businesses do not run themselves. Nor, in most cases, do you run a thriving e-business entirely by yourself. You will almost certainly face the challenge that business owners have faced for centuries: how to attract and hire qualified individuals who can feel the same fire in the belly for your e-business that you feel. This hiring process can well be viewed as the growth tip of your organization, where your energy and commitment to the company flows through to new participants in your enterprise.

1

STEP 11

Manage Your E-Business Team

STEP 11 CONTINUES THE FOCUS ON THE management of human resources, beginning with motivation beyond the paycheck or stock options for e-business managers and employees. What makes an employee a top performer in your e-business? What keeps your best hands from jumping ship? What makes workers want to give their best effort to operations and projects?

Not the paycheck alone. In fact, "throwing money at the problem" to improve performance has proven notoriously ineffective in everything from union negotiations to U.S. foreign policy. Consider two realities of work life:

1 **Almost all workers need more money than they receive.** These needs are far from frivolous. Managers as well as employees are trying to save for their children's college expenses and their own retirements. Workers in the "sandwich generation" find

themselves financially responsible for both their own children and their aging parents. Single parents face child-care expenses that may effectively reduce their take-home salary to minimum wage.

2 **No manager or owner of an e-business can afford always to pay employees what they need.** Take-home pay may meet the bills, but never the needs. Fortunately, workers show up each morning for *more* than the paycheck. Managers who know why this is so are legends in their companies—those rare individuals who spend time and attention on their employees in addition to wages.

The Shrinking Power of Money as a Motivator

WHAT LEVEL OF EMPLOYEE PERFORMANCE AND LOYALTY will your wages buy? Typically, the newcomer to your e-business is more motivated by money, because he or she has built few social bonds at the company, has little ego involvement with long-term projects or planning, and has slight personal identification with the fate of the e-business.

But as the months of employment turn into years, the involvement factor begins to grow as a motivator. Old-timers do work in part for the pay, of course, but there are also at play the many coworker relations, interesting tasks, respect from superiors and subordinates, and that settled-in feeling for the workplace as a surrogate home. (To make this point in an extreme way, consider the e-business owners and managers who have made their fortunes and could retire in luxury but still continue to show up at the office every day.)

It is no exaggeration to say that the primary challenge of every manager is to understand and use the involvement factor as a management tool for growing the company and achieving its mission. Here is an analysis of the components of the involvement factor—what it is, how to use it, and with whom, for e-business success.

FOUR COMPONENTS OF THE INVOLVEMENT FACTOR

ASKING JUST HOW THE INVOLVEMENT FACTOR WORKS IN e-business is an invitation to a quick tour of the four "big discoveries" in employee motivation in the twentieth century. Each of these components can provide workers with an extra incentive beyond the paycheck—with healthy results for the e-business.

1 **The Needs Component.** What do your employees need from their jobs? Psychologist David McClelland and his coworkers approached this question by asking workers to view pictures and then write brief stories about them. Three executives, for example, were individually given a photograph that shows a man sitting down and looking at family photos arranged on his work desk. When asked to write about the picture, one executive wrote about an engineer who was daydreaming about a family picnic the next day. The second executive described a product designer who had his family to thank for his latest bright idea. The third executive saw a structural engineer confidently at work on a bridge-stress problem.

From the evidence provided by thousands of such test samples, McClelland arrived at the three needs workers most commonly expressed:

◆ *Need for achievement.* Workers with a high need for achievement want individual responsibility, frequent feedback, and challenging goals.

◆ *Need for affiliation.* Workers with a high need for affiliation want fulfilling interpersonal relationships at work and opportunities to communicate often with coworkers and clients.

◆ *Need for power.* Workers with a high need for power want to exercise influence over others and gain attention and recognition for their status.

As you consider your e-business workplace, you probably don't need to administer paper-and-pencil tests to determine which employees have particular needs. Managers who know their employees usually have a quite accurate idea of what each employee needs.

The key, then, to motivation through needs is obvious: *give employees what they need.* For example, you can manage a worker with a high need for affiliation by giving him or her liaison, coordinator, or other interpersonal responsibility. The committee or meeting assignment that may sound burdensome and repellent to you will probably sound attractive and motivating to the employee with affiliation needs.

Manage the worker with a high need for power by assigning supervisory responsibility—and expecting results. Manage the worker with a high need for achievement by using the manage-by-objectives approach. Set clear, challenging goals with associated feedback points and rewards for performance.

When e-business managers understand what needs an individual employee has and uses those needs to identify salient rewards, then involvement and motivation will naturally follow.

2 **The Expectancy Component.** A second aspect of the involvement factor stems from what employees expect. A motivated employee will answer "yes" to three questions:

◆ Are you able to perform or accomplish the task?

- Does your performance bring you a predictable result?
- Do you value that result?

If a worker answers "yes" to all three questions, then he or she will be motivated to expend maximum or near-maximum effort on work tasks. But even one "no" answer breaks the chain and minimizes motivation.

Obviously, a manager's goal in an e-business environment should be to ensure that workers can answer "yes" to all three elements of the motivation formula. A manager can affect how each question is answered by (1) providing support and resources so a worker is able to perform, (2) being clear about what rewards employees will receive, and (3) knowing what rewards employees value. In particular, managers must make sure that *performance predictably leads to results that workers value.*

3 **The Equity Component.** A third component of the involvement factor has to do with perceived fairness. Inevitably, workers in e-business compare what they do and receive with what others do and receive in the company. If they feel an inequity as a result of that comparison, that response can become a powerful factor in determining motivational levels. Few other traditional motivators, including salary, reputation, or challenging work, can overcome the deep burn felt by a worker who feels cheated.

The equation for equity is straightforward:

$$\frac{\text{my reward}}{\text{my input}} \quad \text{should equal} \quad \frac{\text{your reward}}{\text{your input}}$$

When the sides of the equation balance, we're satisfied and proceed with work in a motivated way. But when the balance tilts heavily against us, we often show our frustration and sense of injustice.

Managers can prevent equity warfare in the e-business by distributing work responsibilities and related rewards as fairly as possible. Clear differences among employees can be established by distinguishing job titles, job descriptions, chains of reporting, numbers of employees supervised, and types of rewards distributed. In this way, workers have fewer direct points of comparison when evaluating the fairness of their own situations.

4 **The Attitude Component.** The final component in the involvement factor focuses broadly on worker attitudes in relation to motivation.

Employees tend to be most satisfied by:

- achievement
- recognition
- the work itself
- responsibility
- advancement
- growth

By contrast, employees tend to complain most often about:

- company policy and administration
- supervision
- relationship with supervisor
- work conditions
- relationships with peers
- relationships with subordinates

These complaints can be termed "dissatisfiers."

To avoid employee dissatisfaction (and the accompanying lack of motivation), a manager must take care of the dissatisfiers (e.g., fair supervision, adequate work conditions). *But to go to the next step and truly motivate an employee,* a manager must develop a reward system that focuses on the satisfiers. Keep in mind that what is necessary (preventing dissatisfaction) is not sufficient to motivate. A manager's top priority should be to promote satisfiers rather than to remove dissatisfiers. Taking away problems in the form of dissatisfiers does not produce a motivated employee. Only the presence of satisfiers can do that.

FINDING THE RIGHT FIT

NEEDS, EXPECTANCY, EQUITY, ATTITUDE—WHICH MOTIVATIONAL component of the involvement factor best fits employees in your e-business? To which do you respond

Priority of Wanted Job Aspects

(1=HIGHEST)	SUPERVISOR'S RANK	WORKER'S RANK
GOOD WORKING CONDITIONS	4	9
FEELING "IN" ON THINGS	10	2
TACTFUL DISCIPLINE	7	10
APPRECIATION FOR WORK DONE	8	1
MANAGEMENT LOYALTY TO WORKERS	6	8
GOOD WAGES	1	5
PROMOTION AND GROWTH WITH COMPANY	3	7
UNDERSTANDING OF PERSONAL PROBLEMS	9	3
JOB SECURITY	2	4
INTERESTING WORK	5	6

SOURCE: HERSEY AND BLANCHARD, AS CITED IN MOTIVATING PEOPLE, BY DAYLE SMITH (1997)

most powerfully? Managers can answer these questions only by getting to know their employees well and being honest with themselves. It is important for managers not to assume that their own list of motivators is identical with their workers'. As research studies have shown, what's high on a manager's list of motivators may be low on a worker's (see the table above).

Notice in particular that "good wages" ranks number 1 for supervisors but only number 5 for workers. Because a 10 percent raise might send a manager over the moon with joy, he or she might assume that a 10 percent raise would be similarly motivating for an entry-level employee. But remembering that "good wages" was no more than a 5 for workers, it may turn out that entry-level workers raised from \$6.10 to \$6.71 an hour (a 10 percent raise) may not be motivated to work like John Henry. Many Generation X employees, in fact, may yawn.

Especially in a new e-business operating on a dream and a financial shoestring, the involvement factor becomes a crucial set of tools for managers seeking to boost morale and productivity. Payday can become only a part of the effective manager's panoply of motivational strategies—and often not the most important part.

Managing the Integrity of Your E-Business Staff

LET'S SAY THAT YOUR EMPLOYEE TEAM HAS NOW grown substantially. You don't have the day-to-day contact with each of your employees that you used to have. Nor do you have the same level of trust in your employees that you once had. Things are missing, and company resources are being abused. Someone is to blame.

Across industries, up to 85 percent of all theft and fraud stems from employees, not outsiders, according to Department of Commerce estimates. The categories of theft and fraud include the following:

- embezzlement large and small, ranging from felonious robbery to snatching from petty cash and postage
- unauthorized expenses for telephone, fax, computers, company vehicles, and other equipment
- removal of equipment, parts, software, and office supplies from company premises
- fraudulent filing of expense reports and reimbursement requests
- exaggerated or wholly fictitious accident and injury claims
- misuse of days off for sickness or family emergencies
- use of company facilities and personnel for personal business or entertainment, including Internet play and excessive nonbusiness e-mail, voice mail, and overnight mail services
- company-paid travel ostensibly for business but in fact for personal purposes

Consider also these hazy but no less harmful aspects of employee theft and fraud:

- selling company products or services to clients or others "at a special discount" made possible because the employee is trafficking in stolen goods or offering professional services on a moonlight basis in direct competition with your e-business—and often using the very skills you taught the employee!
- taking advantage of company clients and other contacts for personal gain. This can involve inappropriate off-the-clock business dealings with clients, sharing information from

Using the Involvement Factor: Tips for Managers

Motivating by the Needs Factor

- A manager can discern an employee's individual needs by listening and observing.
- The manager's own needs are not a template for determining the employee's needs.

Motivating by the Expectancy Factor

- Employees will devote more effort to achieving goals that they think are attainable.
- Managers must help affect how employees view their ability to do the job.
- For maximum motivation, employees must value the rewards they expect to receive.

Motivating by the Equity Factor

- Managers must know what job titles, duties, and salaries employees are likely to use for comparison with their situations.
- Managers must structure work organizations to prevent unproductive comparisons by workers.
- Managers can control information about jobs and salaries to influence comparisons.

Motivating by the Attitude Factor

- Eliminating poor work conditions does not automatically create a motivating work climate.
- Managers should give priority to providing satisfiers (motivators) and preventing dissatisfiers.

confidential client or company files, and quid pro quo arrangements for favors and considerations.

- tampering with records, computer files, programming, server protocols, schedules, documents, or products in such a way as to discredit a fellow employee, hide one's own misdeeds, or place the company in a bad light.

Whether your e-business involves a handful or dozens of employees, your viability as a business enterprise depends on your ability to prevent employee theft, fraud, and abuse in all forms. This portion of the e-business staffing chapter shows you what to watch for and what to do about it. At the same time, avoid paranoia about your employees' actions and motives. Thieves and cheaters in your workplace probably remain the rare exception, albeit an expensive one.

Focus your energy on preventing theft and fraud. Although obviously necessary, after-the-fact recovery of stolen funds or property and punishment of the guilty usually involves a net loss to the e-business due to executive time, legal expenses, employee turnover and rehiring/training expenses, and perhaps fees to professional investigators. In short, punishment is infinitely more expensive and legally hazardous than is prevention.

WHY SOME EMPLOYEES BITE THE HAND THAT FEEDS THEM

THE VAST MAJORITY OF EMPLOYEES ARE HONEST TO THE POINT of not taking home even pens and paper clips from the company—well, at least not *boxes* of pens and paper clips. But their opposites—those who in one way or another may steal half again their salary or more from you each year—have a variety of rationalizations for their misdeeds. To understand these misguided motives is to prepare and protect yourself against employee theft and fraud:

"Everyone does it." You know, of course, that "everyone" in your workforce does not steal. But thieving employees may have a quite different perspective. They commonly organize themselves in cliques or clusters—the inner circle with whom they share their escapades and tales of what they got away with—then judge what "everyone" does by the low standards of this small group. Watch, therefore, for *theft rings* among your workers. Only rarely does a repeat offender not involve an accomplice or at least a confidant.

"It was small potatoes." Most thieves and cheaters downplay the seriousness of their infractions by an appeal to relative scale: what's a $300 read/write CD drive to a company that makes millions each year, or to a boss who drives a Mercedes? Relative scale should never be accepted to rationalize a permissive attitude toward theft and fraud. Establish a *zero tolerance policy* for theft and fraud in any form or for any amount.

"They had it coming." A significant portion of employee theft or sabotage arises from a felt injustice of some kind. The boss criticizes my work in front of others, so I respond by sticking a $300 copy of Windows 2000 in my briefcase or lunch box to take home. A coworker says something offensive to me, so I strike back at the world in general by anonymously throwing some bugs into the accounting software. Be alert to *anger theft and abuse* in the aftermath of interpersonal conflict, reprimands, or other personnel problems in the workplace.

"I had it coming." Employees who feel undercompensated or unrecognized for their work sometimes respond by a self-devised "bonus" plan. They take home just enough company equipment or money to raise their total compensation to what they perceive as a equitable amount. Studies have shown characteristic patterns for such thefts. They commonly occur in the days immediately before or after payday, then cease almost entirely until the next payday. Guard against this kind of *equity theft or abuse* particularly (1) after an employee has been turned down for a raise or promotion, (2) after a company-wide wage freeze has been established, and (3) during periods of company turmoil (restructuring, takeover, new management, and so forth).

In an era of telecommuting in e-businesses everywhere, employees often "explain away" many de facto thefts as "borrowing"—one of the company's printers may have been found at my home, but I had to keep up with my work, didn't I? I was going to return it. What do you think I am, a thief? Frankly, yes. Don't accept *after-the-fact rationalizations* as excuses for stealing. Employees with a legitimate off-site need for company equipment request it in advance, usually in writing. In advance of any such problem, your policies for removal of equipment from company premises should be clear, specific, and well known to all employees.

SPOTTING THIEVES AND CHEATS DURING THE HIRING PROCESS

CERTAINLY ANY EMPLOYER WOULD PREFER TO FERRET OUT dishonest workers before they sign on to the company payroll. But how do you spot a thief? In the past two decades, one of the great success stories of predicting workplace behavior is the science of *integrity testing*. Foremost among the companies that offer such testing services is Reid Psychological Systems.

For surprisingly inexpensive fees calculated on the number of tests administered, Reid Psychological Systems provides a paper-and-pencil Integrity Attitude Scale comprised of eighty-three questions. Most test takers complete this instrument in about fifteen minutes. Once processed by Reid's computing system, the test reveals with 85 percent classification accuracy which of your job applicants are prone to dishonest statements and acts.

Other tests in Reid's arsenal aimed at potential problem employees are the Safety and Substance Abuse Scale (forty-six questions taking about ten minutes) and a composite instrument, the Abbreviated Reid Report, made up of questions testing integrity, social behavior, substance abuse, and attitudes toward personal achievement (in all, a fifteen-minute test). For further information on scientific approaches to integrity testing, see the several white papers available at www.reidsystems.com/index/htm. You can locate competitors providing similar services on the Internet using the search phrases "integrity testing" and "honesty testing."

Of course, you can also administer integrity tests to employees at any time after hiring. Employers can use test results to plan training or counseling programs or simply to alert supervisors and others to employees with dishonest tendencies.

PROTECTING YOUR E-BUSINESS AGAINST THEFT AND FRAUD

IN ADDITION TO INTEGRITY TESTING, MEASURES TO ELIMINATE employee theft and fraud involve both overt and covert actions on the part of management. Three overt actions are especially crucial, even for an e-business with only a few employees:

1 **Establish specific policies defining fraud and theft within the context of your business,** with discipline procedures clearly spelled out ("up to and including termination and criminal prosecution" is a common phrase in such policies).

Setting the Stage for the Honest Workplace

ANSWER THESE QUESTIONS yourself, then use them to motivate discussion in management meetings and employee briefings.

1 **Who inventories company property?** How often? What happens when items are missing? What records are kept from year to year?

2 **What are your policies about employee theft and fraud?** Where can these policies be located? Are they enforced? Do employees know them well? Do these policies contain clear examples of theft and fraud to prevent any misunderstanding?

3 **To what degree do you consider and/or test integrity as part of hiring and promotion procedures** in your company? Have you investigated integrity testing as part of your selection process?

4 **What part does reinforcement of integrity policies and procedures play in your company's training programs?** In employee publications? In presentations by management to employees?

5 **How much did losses due to employee theft and fraud cost you in recent years?** How much did you spend trying to investigate or prosecute? What legal expenses did you incur in your efforts to deal with employee theft and fraud?

2. **Educate every employee about these policies.** These policies should not be just one more page hidden in your memos, e-mails, or employee manual.
3. **On a monthly or quarterly basis, let employees know about their successes in preventing losses through theft or fraud.** In effect, thank them for partnering with you in maintaining a zero-tolerance policy for such acts. (For comparison, a good model for such notification to employees is the common practice of posting the number of days without a work-related accident. Employees respond positively to a successful track record and work to keep it going.)

6. **What channels of communication now exist in your company** through which employees or clients can anonymously or confidentially report dishonest acts by one of your workers?
7. **Are you getting full-service treatment from your present security agent,** including presentations on security topics to employees and periodic review of security requirements? Or have you settled simply for someone to make sure the doors are locked and the alarms are on?
8. **Do your employees give high or low priority to matters of theft and fraud?** Are such acts tolerated by workers who hear about them? Do workers know what to do when they find out about such acts?
9. **As part of your purchasing program, do you have a reliable system for marking and keeping track** of every piece of equipment, software, furniture, boxes of supplies, computer hardware, and so forth?
10. **What is your own level of commitment to preventing theft and fraud in your workplace?** Are you passionate about this cause, or is it one more item you want to get to when you have more time?

On the flip side, make a big noise when theft or fraud is discovered. If a laser printer disappears from the office, the thief obviously prefers that you shrug it off and sweep the matter under the carpet. Don't oblige the thief!

Finally, three covert policies will help uncover and eventually eliminate employee theft and abuse:

1 **Consider installing video surveillance equipment in main workrooms and equipment storage rooms, computer facilities, and other areas.** A wall-mounted camera and remote monitor can be purchased and installed for well under $500, according to our phone research with several nationwide merchandise outlets including Circuit City, Costco, Office Depot, CompUSA, and others. It's an investment that pays dividends both in what it may reveal about theft and in the stealing and fraud it can prevent.

2 **Contract with a professional security agency to periodically review your internal security measures.** This need not be expensive. You can involve a security expert as an occasional speaker in your employee training program. His or her visible presence will be eloquent and powerful testimony to how seriously you take the problems of theft and fraud.

To link up with this kind of assistance, contact a reputable security service in your area and ask for a free or low-cost inventory of your security needs. Make clear that your central purpose is prevention of theft and abuse, and only secondarily apprehension after the crime. Choose the security firm with the overall plan that best suits your budget and specific security needs.

3 **Investigate lockout options for computers, telephones, and e-mail** to prevent unauthorized long-distance charges, personal business on company time, and legally if not morally hazardous materials finding their way onto company hard drives. When faced with sexual harassment charges or other work-environment issues, many e-companies have found it hard to explain why sexually explicit files had been downloaded from the Internet onto company computers, why e-mail archives contained racist or sexist humor, and why telephone records showed calls from business telephones to adult-only numbers.

By devoting attention and energy to eliminating theft and

fraud in your company, you can protect and improve your bottom line significantly while setting the bar high for what you expect from an honest workforce.

Managing the Security and Growth of Knowledge in Your E-Business

JUST AS YOU MANAGE AND PROTECT THE COMPANY'S PHYSical resources, so you also manage its intellectual resources. Unfortunately, the management of intellectual resources is the weak suit of many managers. By and large, e-business owners and managers are careful people who delight in order. It bothers them when a silly programming glitch snarls traffic at their Web site. They plan their vacations well in advance to avoid gaps in coverage of the office. In short, they manage every part of their e-business with skill—except one. Few manage *knowledge* in any consistent or forward-looking way.

Big Six accounting firms and major business consultants, such as Accenture (formerly Andersen Consulting), have led the way in showing the importance of managing your e-business's knowledge as well as its financial resources. These firms are beginning to offer their clients two revolutionary accounting techniques: knowledge accounting and change accounting. These business advisers have recognized that tracking a company's money, no matter how accurately, still produces only a record of what has worked in the past, not what will work in the future.

These two new forms of accounting and business analysis offer great promise for e-businesses who know that success is determined more by what happens tomorrow than by what happened yesterday. Best of all, these new-wave accounting practices can be learned quickly and applied easily to your e-business's unique circumstances. You don't have to hire a Big Six firm to apply these techniques.

A KNOWLEDGE INVENTORY

WITH A LITTLE DIGGING, YOU CAN PROBABLY ACCOUNT FOR supplies in your office down to the last USB plug. But have you inventoried lately the *knowledge* available in your organization? Don't wilt at the seeming difficulty of the task. Many of our most familiar organizations perform such an inventory regularly. Colleges, for example, inventory their knowledge stores (both in terms of faculty expertise and library holdings) before offering a new program. High-tech companies such as Sun Microsystems and Cisco Systems carefully map out their knowledge holdings before devoting resources to new products or services.

Where can you begin in your e-business to inventory the knowledge you require for continued and increasing success? Take the following five steps, even if only in the form of rough notes in your journal:

1. **List the major areas of knowledge on which your e-business depends for its success.** (Caution: don't simply list knowledgeable people here. Instead, itemize the knowledge stores that your e-business requires for success.) These are your knowledge "support columns." Without them, the enterprise crumbles.
2. **Assign a number (1=low to 10=high) to each of these support columns** to indicate its relative strength or depth in your e-business.
3. **For columns identified with low numbers (i.e., low strength), decide which must be bolstered right away** and which can wait until later for retrofit.

   For columns identified with high numbers (i.e., high strength), decide on the relative resilience or vulnerability of that knowledge. Does it reside primarily in one or two individuals? Begin to think about ways to ensure that the necessary knowledge remains and grows with the organization even if key individuals leave your employ.
4. **Estimate the shelf life of knowledge in your practice.** What seems to be growing stale under the influence of new technologies, materials, products, and techniques? Are the stores of knowledge that have previously ensured your success now outmoded?
5. **Finally, identify employees who are associated with each of your support columns of knowledge**—in effect, create a talent map for your e-business. (One employee may, of course, be linked to several areas of knowledge, as you your-

self probably are.) This mapping exercise will tell you at a glance where you may need to hire or retrain. The talent map may also reveal areas of knowledge redundancy. (More than one e-business has inadvertently attempted to clone the owner through flawed hiring processes.)

In your answers to these queries, you have before you the basis of sound business strategy. In nonfinancial terms, you have quantified and inventoried the real fuel—knowledge—that makes your e-business go. Your financial records are exhaust in the rear view mirror—the byproduct of knowledge at work.

CHANGE ACCOUNTING

YOUR INVENTORY OF THE KNOWLEDGE AVAILABLE IN YOUR e-business reveals not only where you've been but also where you're prepared (or unprepared) to go. Change accounting can help you assess the agility of that available knowledge—in other words, the ability of your e-business to jump when new opportunities present themselves (or to duck when the marketplace starts throwing bricks).

To perform an initial audit of your e-business's change potential, jot down candid answers to these five queries:

1. **What sensing systems are now in place in your e-business to let you know change is in the air?** These sensing systems can involve reading cutting-edge publications, attending relevant conferences, paying attention to the shifting nature of your sector of the Internet, doing competitor intelligence, and, perhaps most important, communicating often and deeply with your employees and customers. Unfortunately, too many e-businesses rely on only one sensing system to signal the need to change: customer falloff or complaints.
2. **How quickly can your e-business acquire necessary new knowledge to transform your company?** What are your primary sources for such knowledge? Should you be exploring new potential sources for knowledge?
3. **How can necessary new knowledge be disseminated quickly and accurately in your e-business?** Is your training program more a ritual than a reality—something you're

always too busy to attend to? Can you rely on it to bring your people up to speed when changes occur in your marketplace or industry?

4 **Finally, who are the "change agents" among your employees—the flexible, imaginative thinkers who can see several moves ahead in the chess game of maintaining a successful, growing e-business?** Probably you yourself come to mind, as you should, along with your partners in the company. Who among this group is empowered to lead when the need arises, or better, well before the need arises? Can the processes, procedures, and rules established for your e-business and its people be relaxed as necessary to free your change agents for creative thinking and action?

By assessing your e-business's available knowledge and its capacity to change, you have equipped yourself with powerful planning tools for making decisions, managing your staff, and nurturing your own growth.

Summing Up Step 11

LET'S ASSUME YOU'VE HIRED WELL. THE DAY-TO-DAY QUESTION for the company leader is now whether you can retain and develop the talent you have attracted to the company. Step 11 shows specific ways in which you can motivate and manage your team. Such efforts take as much commitment as you devoted to technical and business details in shaping your e-business. In a sense, e-business owners prove their durability and character as company leaders by their steady, patient efforts to manage people as well as they manage information systems and other technical matters.

1

STEP 12

Evaluate and Enhance Your Business Model and Web Site Design

THE ONGOING QUESTION FOR A SUCCESSFUL e-business manager is not "Does it still work?" but "Can it work better?" In most cases, the answer to the second question is a resounding "Yes!"

Evaluating Your Web Site

IN INSTITUTING AN ONGOING PROCESS OF SITE evaluation, first recognize that every e-business manager will be grasping at the tail of fleet-footed technologies in the years ahead. Those who hold on and make the most of those technologies will reap the rewards. In the words of Michael Dell, founder of Dell Computers, "In this business, there are the quick and the dead. If you're not quick, you're dead." Internet industry magazines and e-zines (online magazines), books (like this one!), business publications, conferences, trade shows, conversations with other e-business owners and managers, and other informational contacts can expose you to the tornado of advancing technologies in which the Web is now caught up. One handy source for regular e-business updates can be found at www.oracle.com/ebusinessnetwork/. Oracle does a good job of downplaying its commercial interests while highlighting new developments on the Web.

Second, become a bean counter of your Web site statistics. Record and analyze your traffic patterns: When did people tend to visit your site? In response to what factors? (Season, price, ads, and so on.) Profile your visitors: Which site did they visit just before coming to yours? If this sort of data gathering is not your cup of tea, you can turn it over to one of several Web services. In my experience, one of the best of these is SuperStats.com—and the majority of its information-gathering is free.

Below is an overview of SuperStats.com's programs.

Third, stress your site. Take time to put in an order, inquiry, or request that you know will be difficult to process. See where the glitches occur, and repair them. Try to access your site from various browsers. Is your programming working consistently across different browsers, or are you getting funny colors on one and slow response time on another? Test the agility of your Web site during heavy use periods (contact your ISP or domain host for information on when these periods occur in your area).

PricewaterhouseCoopers recently came out with a new software tool for assessing the efficiency of your e-business. Named Emm@ (pronounced "Emma"), the program is targeted to small businesses and offers a multifaceted examination of the enterprise, with reports on management, tax and legal strategies, security procedures, and operations. Learn about Emm@ at www.pwcglobal.com. Says Anthony Tortorici, codeveloper of the program, "It

SuperStats.com's Data-Gathering Programs

	LITE
WHAT I WANT	• Basic tracking (ad based)
IDEAL FOR	• Personal Web sites
HIGHLIGHTS	• Basic reporting • Real-time reporting • Easy setup • Ad-based; button required on your site
PRICING	• Free

helps entrepreneurs identify weaknesses and capability gaps, prioritize initiatives, perform risk assessments, and assess potential business partners."

Evaluating Your People

NEW TECHNOLOGIES AND STRATEGIES HAPPEN THROUGH people or they usually do not happen at all. Jack Deal, a well-known small business consultant, offers these tips for evaluating the human side of your business equation:

- Assess the skills and knowledge of your people. Consider selecting those who are the most computer-literate and express the most interest as leaders to spearhead your Web technology strategy.
- Take a good look at your business strategy and determine what you need in technology to accomplish your company's goals.
- Understand the trends in your industry and factor them into your strategy.

BANNER	PROFESSIONAL
• Complete tracking (ad based)	• Complete tracking (no advertising)
• Small-business sites	• Medium-to-large-business sites • E-commerce sites
• Advanced reporting and visitor profiles • Complete site path analysis • Detailed time on page/ time on site reporting • Real-time reporting • Easy setup • Ad-based; banner required on your site	• Advanced reporting and visitor profiles • Complete site path analysis • Detailed time on page/time on site reporting • Exportable data to PDF, Word, Excel, and Comma delimited files • Real-time reporting • Easy setup • No outside branding or advertising required
• Free	• Monthly $19.95, Yearly $200

- Determine the gap between what you need and what you have. Have your people come up with recommendations.
- Make certain you include personnel training in your IT strategy.
- Train your employees to use the Internet for research.
- Refine your strategy and look for opportunities. Leverage your Web technology strategy to bring increasing value to customers and profits to your company.

Setting Ambitious but Attainable Targets —Then Celebrating Your Success

HOW MUCH TRAFFIC DO YOU WANT TO GENERATE NEXT month? What percentage of those visitors will ask for more information? What percentage will become customers? Where can you trim expenses while maintaining or increasing quality of operations? What verifiable results do you want to see from your next Internet ad or e-mail campaign?

These should not be hope-for-the-best speculations that you mull over on your way to work. Rather, these should be an important part of your daily work discussions and high on your list of priorities. It's a truism that an undefined target is usually impossible to hit. But by regularly letting each of your employees know where the business should be headed, you're giving yourself at least three business advantages:

1. You organize team effort toward a specific goal.
2. You have a basis for evaluating team performance. (Did we make it? If not, why not?)
3. You have a wonderful opportunity for building a "We-can-do-it!" spirit when goals are reached. When they are not reached, you have the basis for a powerful learning experience that will inform your next efforts.

These goals should be written down and publicized in your company. For all the unkind jokes about them, car dealers were on target in their technique of posting how many cars they wanted to sell and how many they had sold day by day. McDonald's does the same thing with number of cars passing through its drive-through service windows. Teams at

McDonald's compete, in fact, to see how many people they can serve in a given time period.

Tracking Customer Satisfaction and Responding to Customer Problems

OUR LIST OF CRUCIAL MANAGEMENT TOPICS CONCLUDES WITH one of the most important: keeping your customers delighted. The formula for business success in e-business has never been a secret:

Capability to provide services + **Availability** of customers who want those services + **Profitability** of pricing or fees = **E-Business Success**

Too often we skip past the all-important second element of this commonsense formula: *What keeps customers available to you?* Customers, in this case, can be considered anyone who makes use of your products or services. The greater your customer satisfaction, the greater your chances for sustained success.

So how much customer satisfaction do you have? In responding to this blunt question, be sure to avoid the following three measurement myths:

- **Myth 1: "I can tell when my customers are satisfied."** In fact, most e-business owners believe what they want to believe, based often on a very limited sampling of real customer feelings. The phenomenon is colloquially called "drinking their own bathwater." For example, the owner of a large Northern California e-business disclosed to me that he had "a feel" for how customers were reacting to his new Web site design: "I can tell by the tone of e-mails we get whether they're happy or not." Trusting such seat-of-the-pants measures of customer satisfaction is professionally hazardous. It is usually only a matter of serendipity how many customers take the time to e-mail a company.
- **Myth 2: "My customers would tell me if there's a problem."** Wounded customers are seldom motivated to help the hound that bit them. They just go away—and tell others. More than one e-business manager has moaned, "Why didn't they e-mail me about the problem?" The cruel fact of

life in this case is that angry customers aren't eager to help you save face or solve your awkward problem. Their anger often expresses itself in efforts to embarrass you professionally, as in chat-room blasts and bulletin-board criticism.

- **Myth 3: "My staff keeps me informed about customer satisfaction."** More accurately stated, your staff probably keeps you informed only about the big stories, pro or con, about your customers. You seldom hear about the smaller incidents and seemingly trivial events involving customers who were disappointed or misserved due to staff mistakes or negligence. Your staff probably communicates most often their tales of personal heroism or martyrdom—but not their tales of failure.

Another cause for a manager's ignorance of customer feelings lies in the delegation process. With good reason, e-business owners often delegate away the dozens of niggly complaints and problems that come in each month. Staff are told "Don't bother me with the little stuff—you handle it." But one unfortunate side effect of such delegation is the manager's growing isolation from the reality of customer attitudes.

AN EAR TO THE GROUND

AN E-BUSINESS OWNER CAN LISTEN TO WHAT CUSTOMERS ARE really saying by paying attention to both the *quantity* and *quality* of their comments. Achieve a reasonable quantity of customer satisfaction information by:

- including a "We care about serving you..." e-mail to customers when they do business with you or, for that matter, when they don't. Design the message for easy reading and, if you wish, response of some kind.
- setting up a feedback e-mail address that customers can use to express their feelings about your products and services. Commit to using the information your feedback center provides to improve your operation and customer relationships. We all resent companies that solicit our opinions and then seem to do nothing with them.
- carrying out a regular, systematic e-mail or regular-mail campaign to determine customer satisfaction levels. You

might decide, for example, to have a staff member e-mail every fifth customer on your order list within two days of providing a product or service of some kind. The contact should be upbeat and to-the-point: "We're contacting you to make sure you were satisfied by your last purchasing experience with us. Would you rate the service you received as excellent, fair, or poor?" Customers may often have to be assured of confidentiality and anonymity for reliable feedback. In sending such messages, avoid the presumption of negative reactions ("Were there any problems...Did you feel dissatisfied by... Have you experienced difficulty with..."). You can easily skew the answers you receive by guiding responses toward negative territory.

Sheer quantity of responses alone is an incomplete measurement of customer satisfaction. You must supplement such data with quality measurement—an in-depth understanding of why customers love you or leave you. This can best be accomplished by a prearranged customer interview or small focus group. Be careful not to select only those customers with whom you've become friendly. Choose a limited number of clients, based on their differing customer profiles, and request a few minutes of their time to chat candidly (perhaps at their site, by e-conference, or by telephone conference) about what they like and dislike about your operation. Let them know that your motive is solely to improve service to them, not to gather evidence against particular employees. Take notes on what you hear and, later, highlight and categorize key phrases and themes.

DRAWING CONCLUSIONS

FROM THE QUANTITY AND QUALITY OF CUSTOMER SATISFACTION information thus accumulated, you can draw reliable conclusions about what to fix, fire, or fumigate in your e-business. Your effort at measuring customer satisfaction pays an additional dividend: you've communicated to your customers that their feelings matter to you and that you are striving to serve them better.

Finally, you have installed a vital new component in your planning and business decision-making processes. By undertaking a survey of customer satisfaction on a regular basis, you can determine whether you and your people are moving forward or backward in efforts to please your client base. Your measurement of customer satisfaction becomes a valuable road map showing the best routes for your e-business to take in the future.

Keeping Your Site Fresh

ALTHOUGH THERE IS VIRTUE IN MAINTAINING THE SAME approximate look of your Web site for the sake of branding, the content within that shell should change frequently. Install, for example, a "What's New?" column where you feature new products or services, special pricing, new hires, and so forth. Perhaps a "What a Deal!" column could include products that you are discounting for fast sale. A "Contest of the Month" column could draw users to enter the contest, then have them back again and again to check who won. An "Information" box or page can be a source of industry information that users cannot easily get elsewhere (for example, application tips for products or health/safety warnings). "News and Views" can be a forum for user questions and feedback. By monitoring this feature, you can edit out silly messages. Do not eliminate all negative comments, however; by answering them directly and helpfully, you increase your credibility and that of your site. A "Guest Columnist" from your industry could write a few paragraphs about industry trends, customer needs, government regulations, or new product applications.

Stepping On

WE'VE CONCLUDED 12 STEPS TOGETHER THAT I HOPE WILL increase your chances for e-business success. The additional resources recommended in Appendix A (*Entrepreneur Magazine's* 100 Best Sites for Business) will take you deeper into many of the topics we have discussed in these pages. The best resources of all, of course, remain your own street smarts and creativity—probably the resources that got you involved in e-business in the first place. No matter how many opinions you consider, including mine, on your e-business journey, remember to listen hard to your own independent judgment. In the great words of the poet William Blake, "No bird flies too high if it flies with its own wings." Good luck!

Appendices

Appendix A

Entrepreneur Magazine's Best Web Sites for Your Business

FIND IT

WITH SO MUCH STUFF ON THE WEB, HOW DO YOU FIND WHAT you need, now? Cut to the chase and check out the best search tools on the Net:

Google (www.google.com). Tied for best search engine, Google has a funny name, but it's a serious hunting tool. Don't miss the "cache" feature, where Google stores pages on its servers. If a site is down, the page may still be readable at Google.

Faster Search & Transfer (FAST) (www.alltheweb.com). The aim of this Norwegian company, the other first-place search engine, is, well, to capture all the Web.

Northern Light (www.northernlight.com). Some of the material is free, some will cost you, but this is fast, intelligent searching.

Dogpile (www.dogpile.com). A meta-search tool, Dogpile simultaneously puts your query to more than ten search engines (from InfoSeek to Google). It's slick, fast, and thorough.

Electric Library (www.elibrary.com). This is still the best site for accessing magazine and newspaper archives, and a thirty-day trial is free; thereafter, it's $9.95 per month for all the articles you can download.

Reprinted with permission from "100 Best Web Sites for Your Business," *Entrepreneur Magazine*, May 2000, <http://www.entrepreneur.com>.

WorldPages (www.worldpages.com). Need a phone number? Go here. There are even resources for finding numbers in dozens of foreign countries.

Deja.com (www.deja.com). The Net is home to thousands of discussion forums. Are they talking about your business? Deja is the fast way to search these groups.

E-COMMERCE

CAN YOU MAKE BIG BUCKS ONLINE? GET THE INFO YOU NEED to plot an online business at these sites:

All Domains.com (www.alldomains.com). Find out about (and buy) international domains here.

Network Solutions (www.networksolutions.com). This is the primary marketplace for registering U.S. domains.

eMarketer (www.emarketer.com). News and tips about the world of e-commerce abound.

Internet Stats.com (www.internetstats.com). How many users and Web sites are there? If it's a stat about the Net, you'll find it here.

WebDeveloper.com (www.webdeveloper.com). This is a one-stop shop for advice and tools for building better Web sites.

Link Exchange (adnetwork.bcentral.com). Now part of Microsoft's bCentral portal for small businesses, Link Exchange remains the Web's best banner-exchange program.

Linkshare (www.linkshare.com). Put money in your pocket by signing up for affiliate status with L.L. Bean, Renaissance Cruises, ToysRUs.com, and other name-brand retailers at this site.

COMPETITIVE INTELLIGENCE

GET THE GOODS ON COMPETITORS, CHECK BACKGROUNDS ON new hires, or buy credit reports on your customers—all by using the Web to locate what you need. Some of this info is free, but most of it costs. Either way, you'll need this info to grow your business, hire the right people, and make sure you get paid.

KnowX.com (www.knowx.com). This savvy engine ferrets through public records and—for about $1 to $5 in most cases—will report on bankruptcies, liens, judgments, and such against both individuals and businesses.

Company Sleuth (www.companysleuth.com). Tell Company Sleuth the names of up to ten public companies, and it will send you regular e-mail reports with breaking news about the targets. SEC filings, press releases, and even rumors get covered in Company Sleuth's convenient filings, and they're free.

Hoover's (www.hoovers.com). The best content is available for a fee, but there's ample free content to be found by anyone surfing in. Research competitors, track stock market performance, and keep tabs on IPOs.

CreditFYI (www.creditfyi.com). Just $14.95 buys you a credit report on a business, delivered in seconds, and much of the data comes from Esperian (née TRW Credit).

Thomas Register (www.thomasregister.com). The premier sourcebook on U.S. and Canadian companies. Print edition and CD-ROM editions each cost $149, but virtually all of it is online—and free to read.

FREE FOR ALL

THE WEB REMAINS THE ULTIMATE DESTINATION FOR SCORING freebies, including the following:

ZDNet Downloads (www.zdnet.com/downloads/hotfiles/free50.html). This is a regularly updated list of the Web's fifty best free downloads.

FreewareWeb.com (www.freewareweb.com). You can download heaps of software here, all free.

Handango (www.handango.com/home.shtml). Offers freeware and shareware for handheld computers and personal digital assistants that you can try before you buy.

Free Forum (www.freeforum.com). Find plenty of freebies here in lots of categories, including Web site creation guides, magazines, and travel brochures.

FreewebCentral (www.freewebcentral.com). Provides free info from all over the Internet, from stock quotes to driving directions.

Office Depot's Office Business Tools (www.officedepot. com). Lots of forms and templates—everything from a start-up checklist to employee time sheets—can be downloaded for free.

Business Owner's Toolkit (www.toolkit.cch.com). More templates and forms are available here for free from publisher CCH.

ROAD WARRIORS

THERE'S NO FASTER WAY TO BOOK TRAVEL ARRANGEMENTS than online, and you'll probably save money, too. Hundreds of Web sites want your business—these are the best:

1travel.com (www.onetravel.com). It's plain-jane (nothing glitzy here), but if you want to make fast travel bookings, this is your place. Don't miss the "fare beater" tool for great air deals.

Cheap Tickets (www.cheaptickets.com). Want even better air deals? Cheap Tickets sells surplus seats, a.k.a. "distressed inventory," at keen prices.

Travelscape.com (www.travelscape.com). Check this one out before checking in to any hotel. This site promises the lowest prices on hotel rooms anywhere, and if you find a cheaper rate, it'll refund you the difference.

PlacesToStay.com (www.placestostay.com). You want a special room, maybe in a bed-and-breakfast or a foreign city? More than 10,000 lodgings are listed here.

MapQuest (www.mapquest.com). Need a map? Print one out at MapQuest, which also offers free point-to-point, turn-by-turn driving directions.

WebFlyer (www.webflyer.com). Are you a frequent-flier-miles junkie? Bookmark WebFlyer. It has tools for online tracking of your points and also notifies you of rewards incentives.

Car Wiz (www.carwiz.com). Car Wiz makes quick work of finding the best deal for the rental car you want in the city where you'll be. Most major outfits are represented here, as well as a few lesser-known companies.

Hot Spots (www.airsecurity.com/hotspots/HotSpots.asp). A frequently updated report on global hot spots—don't leave home without checking in here first.

TRANSMIT IT

SEND A LETTER, TRANSMIT A FAX, SHIP A PACKAGE, SIGN UP FOR a wireless phone—you can do it all smarter, faster, and often cheaper by stopping at these sites:

Point.com (www.point.com). It's no longer optional: you need a wireless phone. Comparison shop for the best deal in your area at this feature-rich site.

eFax.com (www.efax.com). You can't beat this deal—sign up with eFax.com and get a free fax number that sends faxes to you as e-mail attachments. eFax Plus (at $2.95 per month) lets you pick your area code. A voice-mail option is available with both eFax Basic and Plus at no extra charge.

SmartShip.com (www.smartship.com). Compare costs of shipping packages via Airborne, FedEx, UPS, and the post office, and find tools for tracking packages and finding drop-off locations.

Stamps.com (www.stamps.com). Buy postage online—no muss, no fuss.

Get Speed.com (www.getspeed.com). Enter your address and phone number and GetSpeed.com will tell you if DSL or cable Internet access can be had locally—and it offers info on providers and costs.

SHOP UNTIL YOU DROP

WANT DISCOUNTS? YOU'LL FIND THEM ON THE WEB, ON everything from office supplies to computers to automobiles.

mySimon (www.mysimon.com). A leader among "shopping bots," this one prowls the Web for the best prices on the gear you want.

BotSpot (www.botspot.com). Find an index of shopping bots here.

Edmunds.com (www.edmunds.com). Get car and truck reviews and prices.

OutletZoo.com (www.outletzoo.com). When you don't need the latest computer gear, shop here for manufacturers' surplus and refurbished PCs, laptops, and more (most with warranties).

Quotesmith.com (www.quotesmith.com). Shop for insurance—group medical, life, workers' comp, and more—at this easy-to-use site.

Gomez.com (www.gomez.com). Read ratings of e-tailers in many categories, from airlines to computers.

Consumer World (www.consumerworld.com). Get links to nearly 2,000 resources for smart shopping.

HIRE POWER

THE WEB IS AWASH WITH SITES FOR EMPLOYERS SEEKING HELP, as well as for small businesses hunting for independent contractors and consultants to tackle specialty projects. Among the best help-wanted marketplaces are:

Monster.com (www.monster.com). This is probably the biggest online help-wanted site.

HotJobs.com (www.hotjobs.com). HotJobs is positioning itself as a fast-rising competitor for help-wanted ads.

Free Agent (www.freeagent.com). This marketplace links businesses with self-employed independent contractors.

Guru.com (www.guru.com). This site offers another marketplace for finding independent contractors.

GO TO THE PROS

NEED A LAWYER, ACCOUNTANT, OR MAYBE JUST SOME INFORmation on laws or taxes? Get on the Web and find what you want, pronto:

Lawyers.com (www.lawyers.com). Yep, 420,000 lawyers are profiled at this Web site, based on the *Martindale-Hubbell Law Directory*. Searches can be done by name, practice area, location, and more.

Nolo.com (www.nolo.com). You're a do-it-yourselfer? Good luck—and make sure to check the resources at Nolo's self-help law library before making any rash decisions.

FindLaw (www.findlaw.com). Do in-depth legal spadework at FindLaw, where you can search court decisions.

Quicken.com (www.quicken.com/taxes). For do-it-yourself answers to common tax questions, dig here. The info on IRA deductions is especially rich.

MONEY TALKS

DON'T FINANCE BLIND! FIND OUT MORE ABOUT BUSINESS, land-venture, or angel financing at these key Web sites:

Garage.com (www.garage.com). Don't know where to begin your own hunt for venture funds? One of the best sites around for that hunt is Garage.com.

Venture Capital Resource Library (www.vfinance.com). A good site for getting information on the movers and the shakers in the VC world and how deals get cut.

Bankrate.com (www.bankrate.com). Shop for the best terms on bank loans, credit cards, and auto financing here.

Money Hunter (www.moneyhunter.com). This is the home page for the TV show of the same name, which helps entrepreneurs link up with VCs and angels.

LiveCapital.com (www.livecapital.com). Apply online for loans from American Express, Bank of Hawaii, and many more institutions.

REFERENCE DESK

THROW OUT THOSE BULKY REFERENCE BOOKS. INSTEAD, LOOK up meanings of words, flip through encyclopedia entries, and find other information online.

OneLook (www.onelook.com). A massive 597 dictionaries are online here, and all are easily searched.

Britannica.com (www.britannica.com). The leading encyclopedia is online—and free.

Information Please (www.infoplease.com). This is the digital edition of the standard desktop reference.

World Time Zone (www.isbister.com/worldtime). What time is it in Singapore—or anywhere else in the world? A few mouse clicks will tell you.

UNCLE SAM

THE U.S. GOVERNMENT WANTS YOUR BUSINESS TO THRIVE, AND it has set up tons of Web sites with great info and tips. Among the hundreds of sites operated by Uncle Sam, these are tops for entrepreneurs:

Small Business Administration (www.sba.gov). The SBA has set up this gateway page into its many assistance programs for small-business owners.

U.S. Patent and Trademark Office (www.uspto.gov). This is the place to find out whether you're first with that better mousetrap.

Securities and Exchange Commission (www.sec.gov/edgarhp.htm). Search this database of filings made by publicly held corporations, free of charge.

Internal Revenue Service (www.irs.gov). Afraid of the tax man? Get obscure tax forms, information, and even advice from the tax collectors themselves.

U.S. Census Bureau (www.census.gov). This site offers a treasure chest of information on the nation and its people.

Bureau of Labor Statistics (www.bls.gov). Get a snapshot of the labor marketplace—and the nation's economy as a whole—at this terrific government site.

The International Trade Administration (www.ita.doc.gov). Uncle Sam wants to give you the boost you'll need to become a global powerhouse; find plentiful resources here.

Fed World (www.fedworld.gov). This gateway leads you to the reams of statistics and information issued by the federal government and helps you find your way around Fed-land.

WEB TOOLS

NEED TO GET ORGANIZED? WISH YOU HAD OFFLINE STORAGE of critical files? The Web is jammed with servants ready to do your bidding, and everything here is free.

AnyDay (www.anyday.com). Get your calendar online here. Plentiful Web-based calendars exist, but this one syncs with PDAs (like Palms) and PIMs (such as Lotus Organizer). Contacts can be managed here, too.

Evite (www.evite.com). Scheduling meetings is a drag. Even inviting folks to lunch can turn into phone tag. Automate the process with Evite, which sends out invites and keeps you posted on who's R.S.V.P.ed. Enough fun comes built in so that Evite doesn't seem like a nag.

i-Drive.com (www.idrive.com). Here, you'll get off-site data storage for accounts receivable, critical works-in-progress, customer records, and other key info needs in the event of a fire, flood, quake, or anything else that can wipe out a business. How much space at i-Drive? Infinite.

Universal Currency Converter (www.xe.net/ucc). If it's money, head here and you can find out what it's worth.

NEWS YOU CAN USE

WHEN NEWS HAPPENS, THE WEB IS THERE, WITH ONLINE reports surfacing minutes after most notable events. Better still, the Web lets you customize news so you see only what interests you.

My Yahoo! (http://my.yahoo.com). Customize a personal start page with the news you want, built mainly on feeds from Reuters, the international wire service.

1st Headlines (www.1stheadlines.com). 1stHeadlines's mission is to update as fast as news breaks, and it draws from 305 news sources to do it.

BBC (www.bbc.co.uk). The British Broadcasting Corp. is still the top choice for tracking international stories.

Quote.com (www.quote.com). This slick and informative site tracks movement on the stock market.

Weather.com (www.weather.com). From the Weather Channel, this is the place for weather reports.

COMPUTER RX

PLENTY CAN (AND ALL TOO OFTEN DOES) GO WRONG WITH computers. But lots of help is available online—and for free.

Tech Web (www.techweb.com). Find hundreds of helpful articles.

Bug Net (www.bugnet.com). This is the place to go when software misbehaves.

Help for World Travelers (www.kropla.com). Get info about electricity and phone connections abroad.

Updates.com (http://updates.zdnet.com). Get your patches and updates here.

VIRUS WATCH

PRETTY MUCH EVERY E-MAIL WARNING ABOUT VIRUSES IS A hoax, but a few aren't. Before panicking (or deciding to ignore the warning), always check the key sites that track viruses and hoaxes.

Symantec Antivirus Research Center (www.warc.com). If it's a legit virus, news will be reported here, fast. The site also monitors hoaxes. And if you do happen to get a real virus, help is here, too.

AntiViral Toolkit Pro (www.avpve.com). Want a second opinion on that virus alert? Get it here.

Appendix B

E-mail Contacts to Help You Reach Global Markets

Afghanistan
www.afghan-government.com

Angola
www.angola.org/

Argentina
www.undp.org/missions/argentina/

Australia
www.austemb.org/

Bangladesh
www.undp.org/missions/bangladesh/

Belarus
www.undp.org/missions/belarus/

Belgium
www.belgium-emb.org/usa/

Bolivia
www.interbol.com/consul.htm

Bosnia Herzegovina
www.bosnianembassy.org/

Brazil
www.brasil.emb.nw.dc.us/

Cambodia
www.embassy.org/cambodia/

Canada
www.cdnemb-washdc.org/

China
www.china-embassy.org/

Colombia
www.colombiaemb.org/

Costa Rica
www.costarica.com/embassy/

Croatia
www.croatiaemb.org/

Cyprus
www.trncwashdc.org/

Czech Republic
www.czech.cz/washington/

Denmark
www.denmarkemb.org/

Dominican Republic
www.domrep.org/

Ecuador
www.ecuador.org/ecuador/

El Salvador
www.elsalvadorguide.com/consalvamia/

Eritrea
www.usia.gov/posts/eritrea/

Estonia
www.estemb.org/
Ethiopia
www.nicom.com/~ethiopia/
European Union
www.eurunion.org/
Faeroe Island
www.denmarkemb.org/
Finland
www.finland.org/
Georgia
server.parliament.ge/FOREIGN/GEEMB3.html
Germany
www.germany-info.org/
Ghana
www.usembassy.org.gh/
Great Britain
www.britain-info.org/
Greece
www.greekembassy.org/
Greenland
www.denmarkemb.org/
Haiti
www.mnsinc.com/embassy/
Hong Kong
www.hketony.org/
Hungary
www.hungaryemb.org/
Iceland
www.iceland.org/
India
www.indianembassy.org/
Indonesia
www.kbri.org/
Iran
www.daftar.org/
Iraq
www.undp.org/missions/iraq/
Ireland
www.irelandemb.org/
Israel
www.israelemb.org/
Italy
www.italyemb.org/
Jamaica
www.caribbean-online.com/jamaica/embassy/washdc/
Japan
www.embjapan.org/
Jordan
www.jordanembassyus.org/
Kenya
www.embassyofkenya.com/
Kuwait
www.kuwait.info/nw.dc.us/
Kyrgyzstan
www.kyrgyzstan.org/
Laos
www.laoembassy.com/
Latvia
www.seas.gwu.edu/guest/latvia/
Lesotho
www.undp.org/missions/lesotho/
Liberia
www.liberiaemb.org/
Lithuania
www.ltembassyus.org/
Luxembourg
www.undp.org/missions/luxembourg/
Libya
www.undp.org/missions/libya/
Macedonia
ourworld.compuserve.com/homepages/yuembassy/

Madagascar
www.embassy.org/madagascar/
Malaysia
www.undp.org/missions/malaysia/
Maldives
www.undp.org/missions/maldives/
Mali
maliembassy-usa.org/
Marshall Islands
www.rmiembassyus.org/
Mauritania
www.embassy.org/mauritania/
Mauritius
www.idsonline.com/usa/embasydc.html
Mexico
www.quicklink.com/mexico/
Micronesia
www.fsmembassy.org/
Moldova
www.moldova.org/
Monaco
www.monaco.mc/usa/
Mongolia
members.aol.com/monemb/
Mozambique
www.undp.org/missions/mozambique/
Nepal
www.newweb.net/nepal_embassy/
Netherlands
www.netherlands-embassy.org/
New Zealand
www.emb.com/nzemb/
Norway
www.norway.org/
Pakistan
www.pakistan-embassy.com/
Papua New Guinea
www.diamondhead.net/pgn.htm
Peru
www.heuristika.com/consulado-peru/
Philippines
www.philconsul-la.org/
Poland
homepage.interaccess.com/~comconpl/
Romania
www.embassy.org/romania/
Russia
www.rusembus.com/
Rwanda
www.rwandemb.org/
Saudi Arabia
www.saudi.net/
Sierra Leone
amenhotep4.virtualafrica.com/slmbassy/
Slovakia
www.slovakemb.com/
Slovenia
www.undp.org/missions/slovenia/
South Africa
www.southafrica.net/
South Korea
korea.emb.washington.dc.us/
Spain
www.spainembedu.org/
Sri Lanka
www.slembassy.org/
Sweden
www.swedenemb.org/

Switzerland
www.swissemb.org/
Taiwan
www.tw.org/
Thailand
www.thaiembdc.org/
Tunisia
www.ttmissions.com/
Turkey
www.turkey.org/
Turkmenistan
www.dc.infi.net/~embassy/
Uganda
www.ugandaweb.com/ugaembassy/
Ukraine
www.brama.com/ua-consulate/
Uruguay
www.embassy.org/uruguay/
Uzbekistan
www.uzbekistan.org/
Vatican
www.holyseemission.org/
Venezuela
venezuela.mit.edu/embassy/
Vietnam
www.vietnamembassy-usa.org/
Yemen
www.nusacc.org/yemen/
Yugoslavia
ourworld.compuserve.com/homepages/yuembassy/
Zimbabwe
www.zimweb.com/embassy/zimbabwe/

U.S. Embassies Abroad

Argentina
www.hq.satlink.com/usis/
Armenia
www.arminco.com/homepages/usis/
Australia
www.csccs.oze-mail.com.au/~usaemb/
Austria
www.rpo.usia.co.at/
Azerbaijan
www.usia.gov/posts/baku/html
Bahrain
www.usembassy.com.bh/
Bangladesh
www.citechco.net/uskhaka/
Barbados
www.usia.gov/posts/bridgetown/
Belarus
www.usis.minsk.by/
Belgium
www.usinfo.be/
Belize
www.usemb-belize.gov/
Benin
eit.intnet.bj/cca/
Bolivia
www.negalink.com/usemblapaz/
Botswana
www.usia.gov/abtusia/psts/bc1/wwwhmain.html
Brazil
www.embaixada-americana.org.br/
Bulgaria
www.usis.bg/

Canada
www.usembassycanada.gov/
Chile
www.rdc.cl/~usemb/
China
www.redfish.com/USEmbassy-China/
Colombia
www.usia.gov/posts/bogota/
Costa Rica
www.usembassy.or.cr/
Côte d'Ivoire
www.usia.gov/posts/abidjan/
Croatia
www.open.hr/com/ae_zagreb/
Cuba
www.usia.gov/posts/havana/
Cyprus
www.americanembassy.org.cy/
Czech Republic
www.usis.cz/
Denmark
www.usis.dk/
Dominican Republic
www.usia.gov/posts/santodomingo/
Ecuador
www.usis.org.ec/
Egypt
www.usis.egnet.net/
El Salvador
www.usinfo.org.sv/
Eritrea
www.usia.gov/posts/eritrea/
Estonia
www.usislib.ee/usislib/
Finland
www.usis.fi/
France
www.amb-usa.fr/
Georgia
www.sanet.ge.usis/mission.html
Germany
www.usia.gov/posts/bonn.html
Ghana
www.usembassy.org.gh/
Great Britain
www.usembassy.org.uk/
Greece
www.usisathen.gr/usisathens/
Grenada
www.spiceisle.com/homepages/usemb_gd/
Guinea
www.eti-bull.net/usembassy/
Hungary
www.usis.hu/
Iceland
www.itn.is/america/
India
www.usia.gov/posts/delhi.html
Indonesia
www.usembassyjakarta.org/
Ireland
www.indigo.ie/usembassy-usis/
Israel
www.usis-israel.org.il/
Italy
www.usis.it/
Japan
www.usia.gov/posts/japan/
Jordan
www.usia.gov/posts/amman/
Korea
www.usia.gov/posts/seoul/

Kuwait
www.kuwait.net/~usiskwt/wwwhemb.htm
Laos
www.inet.co.th/org/usis/laos.htm
Latvia
www.usis.bkc.lv/
Lebanon
www.usembassy.com.lb/
Lesotho
www.lesoff.co.za/amemb/embassy.html
Lithuania
www.usis.lt/
Luxembourg
www.usia.gov/posts/luxembourg.html
Malaysia
www.jaring.my/usiskl/
Mali
www.malinet.nl/cca/
Malta
www.usia.gov/posts/malta.html
Mauritius
usis.intnet.mu/
Mexico
www.usembassy.org.mx/
Moldova
usis.moldnet.md/
Mozambique
www.info.usaid.gov/mz/
Nepal
www.south-asia.com/USA/
Netherlands
www.usemb.nl/
New Zealand
www.usia.gov/posts/wellington/
Nicaragua
www.usaid.org.ni/
Nigeria
www.gsi-niger.com/cca-usis/
Norway
www.usembassy.no/
Oman
www.usia.gov/posts/muscat/
Pakistan
www.usia.gov/posts/karachi/
Palestine
www.info.usaid.gov/wbg/
Panama
www.pty.com/usispan/
Peru
www.rcp.net.pe/usa/
Philippines
www.usaid-ph.gov/
Poland
www.usaemb.pl/
Portugal
www.portugal.doc.gov/
Qatar
www.qatar.net.usisdoha/
Romania
www.usis.ro/
Russia
www.usia.gov/posts/moscow.html
Senegal
www.usia.gov/abtusia/posts/SG1/wwwhemb.html
Singapore
home1.pacific.net.dg/~amemb/
Slovakia
www.usis.sk/
South Africa
www.usia.gov/posts/pretoria/
Spain
www.embusa.es/

Sri Lanka
www.usia.gov/posts/sri_lanka/
Sweden
www.usis.usemb.se/
Switzerland
www.itu.int/embassy/us/
Taiwan
www.ait.org.tw/
Thailand
www.usa.or.th/
Turkey
www.usis-ankara.org.tr/
Ukraine
www.usemb.kiev.ua/
United Arab Emirates
www.usembabu.gov.ae/
Uruguay
www.embeeuu.gub.uy/
Uzbekistan
www.freenet.uz/usis/
Venezuela
www.usia.gov/posts/caracas/
Vietnam
members.aol.com/nomhawj/
embassy/home.htm
Yugoslavia
www.amembbg.co.yu/
Zambia
www.zamnet.zm/zamnet/
usemb/

Appendix C

Emerging Guidelines for Web Site Compliance with the Americans with Disabilities Act (ADA)

WHEELCHAIR-ACCESSIBLE RESTROOMS. BRAILLE ELEVATOR instructions. Entrance ramps. These are the most familiar signs of compliance with the requirements of the Americans with Disabilities Act (ADA).

But you may not know about the newest wrinkle in ADA requirements for the workplace. Although not yet codified as law, the latest ADA thrust involves your business Web site. Bank of America is now under threat of lawsuit unless it makes good-faith efforts to make its Web site accessible to Americans with disabilities, particularly those people with visual, hearing, motor skill, or cognitive/neurological disabilities. Rumor has it that B of A has spent hundreds of thousands of dollars to date in revising its Web site. (You can see the results at bankofamerica.com.) Wells Fargo Bank is undertaking a similar overhaul of its Web site.

This new development in ADA compliance is being driven by the World Wide Web Consortium (W3C), with bases at MIT, Keio in Japan, and INRIA in France. (It is important to note that this interest group is not involved in or pursuing legal action against companies to encourage or enforce its initiatives.) The W3C is a vendor-neutral advocacy group made up of approximately 400 organizations. Its Web Accessibility Initiative (WAI) has received substantial funding from the U.S. National Science Foundation, the U.S. Department of Education's National Institute on Disability and Rehabilitation Research, the European Commission, IBM, Lotus Development Corporation, Microsoft, and NCR. The group's Web site (compliant, by the way) can be found at www.w3.org/WAI.

The guidelines urged by this group do not have the status of law at present. In the near future, however, it is highly likely that many of these guidelines will be enforceable under ADA regulations, as lawsuits against major companies establish legal precedents. Therefore, it's not too soon to understand what changes you may be making to ensure that your business Web site is accessible to Americans with disabilities.

Here are specific tips for inspecting your Web site with an eye toward coming ADA requirements:

- **Look at the images without alternative, explanatory text on your Web site.** Could an automated "reader" for blind people convey menu items or other site options, or are such choices limited only to the sighted?
- **Examine the "image map hot spots"** (areas on your Web site that will respond to a mouse click). Have you provided text so that visually impaired users can find these spots?
- **Consider any audio or video aspects of your Web site** that are unaccompanied by captions or text descriptions. Can deaf or blind users access the information contained in these portions of your site?
- **Take a hard look at your use of tables, graphs, or charts** that are difficult to decipher when presented in linear form (as they must be when "translated" for blind users).
- **Get to know how well the programming of your Web site adapts** to current screen readers and voice recognition technologies available to Americans with disabilities.

These are but a few of the many suggestions offered by the WAI. You can find a complete list, along with many free resources and compliance tools, at the WAI Web site (cited above).

The underlying argument for undertaking such Web site revisions obviously goes beyond protecting your business from lawsuits at such time that Web site accessibility is given legal status under ADA legislation. The WAI estimates that the percentage of people with disabilities ranges between 10 percent and 20 percent in many populations. Although some of these disabilities (such as heart conditions, difficulty walking, and so forth) do not affect Web accessibility, many other disabilities do.

As e-business, e-education, e-applications, and e-information become mainstream ways of living and learning, people with disabilities have an especially critical interest in removing access barriers to the Internet. The "digital divide" can separate people with disabilities from an increasingly powerful source of business contact and information. Traditional sources of information such as print media are often less accessible to these people, making the Internet even more important as their portal for business and social interaction.

The early test cases for such compliance have involved large banks, as highly visible, regulated organizations with significant expertise in technology. But when voluntary push comes to legislated shove for Web accessibility in American business, all professional and commercial Web sites will be under scrutiny for compliance.

Will such efforts break the budget? Not at all, says the WAI: "Designing a new site to be accessible should not add significantly to development cost.... For existing sites, the ease or difficulty of making sites accessible depends on a variety of factors, including the size of a site, the complexity of a site, and the authoring tool that was used to make a site.... When compared with the broader audience that a site is available to, and the greater usability for other users as well, accessible sites can be cost-effective."

To sum up, you're not required by law to do anything about Web site accessibility at this moment. But for businesses and professionals who like to look at the road ahead, there's good legal and ethical sense in beginning to explore Web accessibility issues. An excellent first step is to read through the dozens of pages of well-developed information at the WAI Web site.

Index

About the Author

Dayle M. Smith holds her Ph.D. in organizational communication from the University of Southern California. Currently she is professor of management at the University of San Francisco, where she teaches courses in leadership, organizational behavior, human resource management, global management, and other management electives in the Executive M.B.A., M.B.A., and undergraduate programs. An active consultant, Smith has worked with a number of firms including Northern Ireland Small Business Institute, Nippon Telephone and Telegraph, China Resources, Charles Schwab & Co., Infogenics, Quaker Oats, WEBB 99, Marriott Corporation, IDG Publishing, Ferrari Foods, American Stores, Colonial Williamsburg Foundation, DuPont-Mexico, Kaiser Health Plan, PaineWebber, Countrywide Mortgage Banking, Cost Plus World Market, and others. Smith is the author of numerous other books concerning business and the workplace. She lives in the San Francisco Bay Area with her husband, two daughters, and golden retriever.